WHAT FILM SCHOOLS DON'T TELL YOU

YOUR BASIC GUIDE TO MAKING MOVIES AND FINDING GOOD DISTRIBUTION

KELLY SCHWARZE

In Memory of Greg Schwarze

WHAT FILM SCHOOLS

DON'T TELL YOU

YOUR BASIC GUIDE TO MAKING MOVIES

AND FINDING GOOD DISTRIBUTION

KELLY SCHWARZE

Published by Indie Film Factory, LLC
3111 South Valley View Blvd E-127
Las Vegas, Nevada 89102

ISBN: 978-0-578-46195-3

This book is dedicated to Charisma, who has been the driving force in my career. She has inspired me to be more, to do more, and to take action! Without her, neither this career nor this book would be possible.

TABLE OF CONTENTS

Introduction

Before I start this book, I want to say that it is my primary goal to help independent moviemakers. More than anything, I aim to offer a practical, easy-to-use workbook to empower content creators to profit from their endeavors. It is the intention of this text to offer some tools and share knowledge that I have gathered over the last twenty years in this business. This book provides the evidence that you don't need "Hollywood" or tremendous amounts of capital to start your film enterprise. The key is to get started.

Many first-time filmmakers get stuck with the budget of their films. In fact, budget insecurity prohibits many film students from making their first feature movie. People waste time looking for money to make movies. When the filmmaker falls short, they typically postpone it indefinitely and talk about it forever.

Wouldn't it would be easier to bring the production down to your financial needs to at least get things rolling?

The biggest problem with film school is that it doesn't teach you how to get started. People seem to think that they need tons of money to start their film careers. This is absolutely false.

Filmmaking used to be an elitist art. Less than twenty years ago, making an indie movie was more expensive than buying a car. If you wanted to make a film, you either needed to be rich, know rich people, or have entertainment connections.

The good news is, the playing field has leveled. Now, any person with a camera and internet connection can create a visual story and share it with the masses.

The information throughout this book compiles everything that I have learned over the course of my career. Moreover, the steps you will be presented have been applied in practice and have guided me from being a dreamer to a doer—and have allowed me to say this: although I have had some amazing support along the way, I started my filmmaking journey with no money, no equipment, and no film-school diploma.

I am hoping this book can create a new conversation within our industry. I aim to help people keep things simple and get back to the basics of good old-fashioned storytelling. Simplicity has allowed me to make movie after movie without having to compromise my creative integrity or financial means. Simplicity has helped me grow my business and has allowed me to flourish as a filmmaker.

I have spent my entire adult life trying to simplify the art of the motion picture. In effect, the idea to create a simple and straightforward system is the most overlooked aspect of filmmaking education. Without pressing this issue too much, I am supplying the following information as a guide to help you get your ideas into action...right now!

If you want to be a moviemaker, then be a moviemaker. Stop wasting time looking for a job, a handout, or a favorable break. This book is designed to help you create your own job and your own favorable break. By taking the time to map out your film career, you will go a long way in creating the kind of action you need to get moving. Don't wait for permission to start. Go!

The text in this book is not written to entertain. This information is a step-by-step workbook for making your movie. It is required that you follow these steps in order. Give yourself plenty of time to effectively accomplish each chapter of this book before you move on. It is also suggested that if you do not fully understand the information in a chapter, go back, review, and reread until you comprehend. Failure to do so will render this book useless for you.

Within this text, you will find the following areas of study:

- **Development of a screenplay**

- **Breaking down your script**

- **Finding locations**

- **Casting your talent**

- **Building your shot list**

- **Making your movie with less (no need**

- **for investors)**

- **Finding distribution**

I hope you find this information inspiring, and if there is anything I hope you get out of this text, it is this: just take action! Don't wait for the conditions to be perfect. Make your own conditions and get going. Believe in yourself and never stop until you complete your movie.

CHAPTER 1

From Dreamer to Doer

Around the age of nineteen, I had my first management job. I was the manager of a small amusement park about fifteen miles from the Las Vegas Strip. At that time, I was focused on two things: getting through college and finding a job in the entertainment industry. I remember one hot summer morning, the general manager made a surprise visit. Like most of the employees that day, I was on pins and needles, hoping that he didn't see any imperfections with our work. He was a stern taskmaster with a reputation for firing people without flinching. I tried to hide as much as I could. I did my best to avoid any interaction that would jeopardize my hard-earned day job. After all, it was the only thing helping me pay my way through college.

Despite my attempts to go unnoticed that day, Mr. Sullivan had cornered me inside the management office while I was breaking change for the cashiers. Mr. Sullivan was an older man, well into his seventies, and spoke with a deep, authoritarian voice. He politely asked me to have a seat. I was beside myself, ransacking my memory bank, trying to figure out what I had done wrong. As I sat there, anxious to escape, Mr. Sullivan leaned back in his chair and stared at me for a few seconds.

"What are your career goals?" he asked calmly.

I sat and pondered for a moment, not sure how to respond.

"Well, I am hoping to make movies someday," I reluctantly replied.

"Do you have any backup plans?" he asked.

It took me a moment to consider the question. I was certain my response would make me look like a young, foolish kid. I hadn't given that question much thought.

"No. Not really," I replied.

To my surprise, Mr. Sullivan folded his arms and leaned back even farther in his chair. I braced for the humiliation. Then, something unexpected happened. As I sat nervously awaiting a grown-up lecture, a smile slid out from under his gray, pencil-thin mustache.

"That's excellent. Just what I hoped you'd say," he responded.

I couldn't believe what I was hearing.

"You should never have a backup plan," he explained. "Backup plans are for failure when it comes to your career goals. You just make it happen, no matter what!"

Little had I known at the time, that moment was a life-changing experience. It not only made more sense to me as time went on, but it has become my personal mission statement. Why create alibis for failure? Why create safety nets for falling short? The idea of only winning, no matter how many times you fail, is a concrete philosophy that I have employed in just about every task I undertake.

A few years later, I was given some bad news from an art school in San Francisco: my financial aid wasn't enough to cover a semester of courses. I was unable to continue my studies. Dejected and beaten by this setback, I reluctantly boarded a plane back to my home town, Las Vegas. I sat on the plane wondering about my uncertain future. Then suddenly I remembered what my old boss had said. As the plane started its ascent, a flash of inspiration swept across my soul. "Rather than trying to figure out how to work around my setback by creating a backup plan, why not list my end goals? A set of goals that would define the term success to me." I immediately grabbed a ballpoint pen from my backpack and jotted down six goals on a drink napkin:

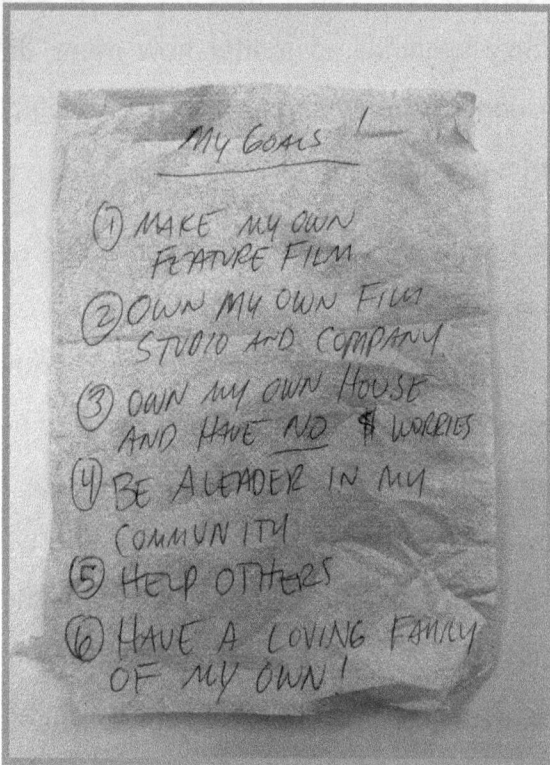

1.   ***Make my own feature film***

2.   ***Own my own film studio and***

3.   *production company*

4.   ***Own my own house and have no***

5.   ***money worries***

6.   ***Be a leader in my community***

7.   ***Be able to help others***

8.   ***Have a loving family of my own***

I am happy to say that I accomplished all of these things without the help of any film school, Hollywood break, angel investor, or charity. In fact, I have checked the first one off seven times and have ultimately achieved all the things that I wanted to do. And, despite having numerous setbacks after the experience in San Francisco, I kept at it, never making back-up plans, never skewing from the things I was most passionate about.

It is fundamentally important to stress that I never knew exactly how I was going to achieve those things at the time. Although I did know that I was determined to take the first few steps to get moving. I never worried about who was judging me or if I was doing things the wrong way. I just did it.

After I returned from San Francisco, I enrolled in the University of Nevada Las Vegas (UNLV) Film Studies program. At that time, the program was still in its infancy. It frustrated me that there was more lecturing than shooting of movies. After my sophomore year, I dropped out of the program and went to work as a production assistant for a Warner Brothers Television show, and while working on the set, I finally realized what I needed to start my career...I needed my own camera!

I saved up as much money as I could, and then I maxed out a store credit card to purchase my first video camera. People around me thought I was nuts. I had spent all that money for a camera that—at the time—was seen as a gimmick. I even had film-school friends tell me that digital video would never take off. One film person I met told me that I wasn't a filmmaker unless I was shooting on film. Nonetheless, I was determined to make my own feature film, and the only way I could see myself creating movement toward that goal was owning a camera that I could afford to shoot with.

A few months later, I rounded up two of my high-school buddies to form a production company called Vision Dynamics Entertainment. A few months after incorporating, we called in several favors to make our first feature movie. The project was a train wreck, but despite that, we finished! We premiered our little movie to a packed theater of family and friends. We sent out press releases to local newspapers and ended up featured in the news. Our small movie event helped put us on the local map as young filmmaking entrepreneurs. In fact, we even had a legendary television director attend our screening. The movie received generous praise from the audience. We also caught the attention of a producer, with whom I would later make two movies.

When I look back at my twenty-plus years as a filmmaker, I can't think of any particular moment where it all came together for me at once. My success overall has been a series of small moments where one thing led to another. It's impressive to see how far I've come. Taking that step in buying my first camera was my catalyst. If I had taken the advice of my critics, who knows where I would be? Perhaps I'd still be *talking* about making my first movie.

The moral of this chapter is to listen to your heart. Just make your damn movie! Don't wait until the conditions are perfect, or to have all the money. Don't hesitate, and certainly do not listen to the critics afterward. Keep plugging along, taking new steps every day until you fulfill your goals. Do not let the actors' unions, grumpy old grip guys, trust-fund kids, or fancy industry hotshots intimidate you. Step forward with pride and self confidence. You will surely make mistakes and fall flat, but use those moments for self-reflection and growth. And always remember that filmmaking is not a career. It is a lifestyle. Never give up

14

your lifestyle. It's who you are. Live with it. Flourish with it. Share it. Die with it.

CHAPTER 2

A New World of Filmmaking

I started my career nearly twenty-two years ago. Like some of you reading this book, I had grand dreams of being a Hollywood superstar. It was my aim to direct multi-million-dollar movies. I aimed at being placed in the same conversations as my heroes, Spielberg, Coppola, and Rodriguez. But as I approached my midthirties, something dawned on me; the myth that is Hollywood is just that, a myth!

It's a myth that we create for ourselves. It consists of the idea that success (in this business) is solely tied to fame and fortune.

As I got older and wiser and started to learn more about filmmaking around the world, I discovered that true filmmaking success is being able to make great stories, no matter the budget, and making movies when you want to, all while still being able to provide a good life for yourself and your family.

In my twenty-plus-year career, I have written, directed, and produced six feature films. I am currently working on my seventh. I have written, directed, and produced scores of commercials (both locally and internationally), music videos for legendary performers, and advertorials for some of the biggest brands in the world. I have helped build successful production companies and have managed to become one of the leading filmmaking voices in my community. I have my own production studio where I can create freely, and I am surrounded by amazingly talented people. I have been to tons of red carpets, mixed it up with the rich and famous, and have had many moments in the spotlight. My network of mentors include Academy- and Emmy Award–winning legends. I have access to some of the biggest shakers in the industry, and yet I have never profited from any Hollywood studio, nor been given favorable breaks by anyone, including all the cool people I know!

I have never made a movie in Hollywood. In fact, all six of my films were movies that I either coproduced or self-financed. Yet most of my titles have seen worldwide distribution, and some have gone on to win awards and have been placed on the same shelves as many other major studio movies.

The thing is, all of *my* movies were ones that I wanted to make, and I have managed to maintain creative control over every aspect.

Interestingly enough, my entire body of work could be budgeted in less than one Hollywood-catering budget and, most importantly, my movies have gone on to earn money: I have seen the rewards for keeping my budgets as close to zero as possible.

If I had to decide which filmmaking example inspires me the most, it would be that of Francis Ford Coppola. Coppola, despite his major successes, has lived a remarkably out-of-the-spotlight career. He forged his own company, American Zoetrope, nearly fifty years ago. He has spent a great deal of his life promoting the talents of others, not only within his family, but with other creatives around the world. What's even more remarkable about Francis Ford Coppola, is that even working outside of the Hollywood system, he has still managed to put out exceptional movies and timeless classics. His career should be a great benchmark for any independent filmmaker. It's certainly something I aim to simulate.

Back in the late nineteen-nineties, there were few resources out there for filmmakers. If you wanted to make a movie, you had to have buckets of money and celluloid.

Today, cameras are better and technology has made making movies easier, faster, and less expensive, and yet, it is amazing to me how many aspiring filmmakers are still fixated on million-dollar budgets and unrealistic goals that typically stifle their abilities to create anything.

Let's face it, the Hollywood dream is dead. The notion of making a movie in Hollywood is almost as possible as being able to fly like one of its superheroes. The industry that we all once aimed to be a part of has changed over the last thirty years, though its myth still manages to string many young creators along.

Since the late 1980s, many of the studios have traded hands many times. They have been owned by electronics' companies, oil barons, alcohol companies, and even foreign governments. Today, much of Hollywood is controlled by major multinational corporations, and the business has moved farther away from a theatrical-entertainment model to a subscription platform and brand-licensing industry. There are many reasons for this.

The market is changing quickly. The demand for high-value ancillary properties is through the roof. There are several emerging economies across the globe, such as China, and that market is demanding familiar American brands at rapid rates.

Moreover, the cost of making and marketing entertainment has gone up nearly double since the 1990s. The risk factor is more than triple what it once was. With so much risk, entertainment Goliaths like Disney and Sony have staked their futures on the ownership of major brands. Large brands offer more consumer value in other sectors of the business, including franchising, video games, merchandise, travel, toys, and, of course, sequels.

To offset the risk of a movie flopping, studios are betting the farm on brands that have great track records and huge built-in ancillary value. Additionally, Hollywood is also in need of new content that has global appeal. With emerging markets like Asia, film studios need to craft content that can appeal across languages and borders.

Over the last decade, Hollywood has taken very little risk on fresh ideas. The rate of original (spec)

21

screenplays purchased by major studios has dropped substantially, according to a *Los Angeles Times* article dated January 19, 2018. And, although there is still hope for budding screenwriters, the heyday for original optioned content has ended.

On the flip side, companies like Amazon, Netflix, and Hulu have picked up the reins and have invested substantially in new ideas and storylines. Their business operates in tonnage. The more titles they have, the more they can charge their subscribers. Plus, these platforms have to spend ungodly sums to recruit the best talent to help them win Emmys and Oscars. What's great about this new system is that even though companies like Amazon and Netflix are going for critically acclaimed prestige, they still have windows of possibility for aspiring new voices in the industry.

For filmmakers like you and me, it's a wasted effort to go fishing in that big Hollywood-studio pond. If you want to make a go at ol' Hollywood, you would be better advised to learn law and economics and try to get a job within a studio-finance department. I have several friends and colleagues who have left to pursue a career in Hollywood and have yet to direct their own films, or to even have their screenplays produced. Hollywood is great for getting a job, but not for making your movies.

Now let me be clear, in this book I am not talking about short films. I'm talking about feature-length movies that are between seventy-five and ninety minutes in length. These are products that you can potentially sell in the marketplace as commercial feature films. These films would include both classic fictional narrative and documentary features. And although short films are starting to find value in the marketplace, I wish to focus this book on feature-length movies. Moreover, this book is not intended to represent larger-scale movies from $250,000 and up. These types of movie projects are in a different class altogether and deserve a different set of strategies and planning. This book is intended for anyone looking to make a movie with a "micro budget" between $10,000 and $100,000.

Most of the topics in this text pertain directly to the goal of scripted and classic-narrative storytelling. However, the portions regarding distribution and development can also apply to documentaries. These chapters can serve not only as a guide for your filmmaking career, but as an entrepreneur. Building a brand and creating product is the goal of this information. I will offer my perspective on what has worked for me and what hasn't.

The other component of this book is that we're going to assume that you are primarily self-funded. It's also my assumption that you have, or can at least secure, roughly $30,000–$50,000 to make a movie. Although I've mentioned this book is specifically designed to talk about budgets up to $100,000, it is my goal to get you to think even smaller.

For me, the perfect budget range is around $30,000–$50,000. However, my first two movies cost roughly $15,000 each. These days my budgets are typically $45,000. This allows me to make a quality, low-budget movie and pay everyone involved. Of course, small budgets like these have their limitations, but if you can learn to develop content well at this budget level, you can not only make money back on your investment, but you can also keep making movies.

Over the last few years, I've been asked a lot about the $30,000 budget range. I actually like that number more and more each year. It sounds ridiculous to some people, especially people coming from the Hollywood mindset. They think, "How can you make a movie for $30,000?" Well, I've done it, and there would have been very little difference in the outcome of these movies had I made them for $100,000. My third feature cost my partner and me around $72,000. This movie was a SAG-modified low-budget agreement. The movie was never sold. We needed an additional $25,000 to buy our way out of the agreement in order to get distribution. No one wanted to give us an advance, so we shelved the movie. It has never been officially released. I could have done that same movie for $20,000 nonunion and not only got distribution, but probably would have made my money back. You see my point?

I'm learning that the closer you keep your budgets to zero, the more effective you'll be as an entrepreneur. The reason for this is very simple. In today's indie-film marketplace, there is little difference between people making $250,000 movies and those making movies costing $10,000–$30,000. The buyers are all the same, and everyone's competing for the same attention on video-on-demand platforms and broadcast.

The punchline is that you want to try to keep your budgets very, very low. Do not get caught up with the notion that your budget range reflects your talent as a content creator. Storytelling is a gift. Good stories will find their way to success regardless if they are unionized or not, or if they were filmed on a digital single-lens reflex camera (DSLR) vs. an Alexa. Good storytelling outweighs the importance of budget. Now surely budget plays a major factor in your ability to tell certain types of stories within a particular market expectation, but do not be fooled. Practice the art of telling stories with less, so you can become a valuable resource for distributors and other producers looking to hire you.

So let's begin.

CHAPTER 3
Finding the Right Material

The first thing I want to talk about is your screenplay. A lot of moviemakers are so eager to get into production that they miss the most important aspect of the process. For me, the most important aspect of the movie process is having a solid script! *Now, what am I talking about, a solid script?* There are a lot of variables that go into the term *solid script*.

I would define *solid script* by the following criteria:

1.   **a well-written work, good dialogue, a fresh idea, and a different twist on a familiar theme**

2.   **A script with a limited number of locations and production headaches**

3.   **A script or idea that fits one of the more popular genre molds: action, suspense thriller, horror, sci-fi, children/family**

28

4.   A screenplay with a limited cast count

5.   A project you can self-produce and finance between $30,000 and $50,000

6.   A script between 75 and 80 pages

So, let's explore each of these.

A well-written work

Over the last few years, I have had some amazing experiences. At our studio, Indie Film Factory, we offer rental space to others looking to do things. On one occasion we had the rare ability to host a screenwriting workshop with University of California at Los Angeles (UCLA) screenwriting professor Bill Boyle. At that time, I had already written and produced a handful of movie scripts. However, I was interested in learning to craft a better visual experience for my writing. What was so great about this experience is that

I didn't have to go anywhere; the workshop came to me.

Mr. Boyle had also written a screenwriting book entitled *The Visual Mindscape*, which I highly recommend you purchase. Mr. Boyle spent the better part of his lecture dissecting two of the greatest screenplays of our generation: *Usual Suspects,* by Christopher McQuarrie, and *Quills,* by Doug Wright. In each instance Mr. Boyle showed clips from the movies and referenced the scripts. Astonishingly to me, both screenplays nearly mirrored the finished cuts of the movies shot for shot. Both McQuarrie's and Wright's scripts had been written more like a descriptive and emotional shot list rather than stage directions for actors.

The experience in Mr. Boyle's class was profound. I immediately went back to work on my script and transformed what started out as a mediocre action caper into a fast-paced and action-packed indie screenplay that nearly got picked up by a major studio.

Since then I have applied *The Visual Mindscape* technique to all my works, including my novellas, and have impressed some of my Hollywood-producer friends.

Whether you are hiring someone to write a screenplay, or wearing that hat yourself, you should aim to make your material as *shoot-ready* as possible. I used to never consider myself a screenwriter. But with these techniques, I feel I can transform mediocre drafts into shoot-ready scripts. Writing this way allows me to convey cinematic expression, while offering a roadmap to shooting the movie.

Below are two different samples demonstrating what I'm talking about. I cannot assume to be an expert on Bill Boyle's technique, but I can share with you what I understand from his teachings. These samples are designed to help you visualize what I'm referring to when I say a *well-written screenplay*. It's not to say that this way is better than any other, but I would encourage you to either write, find, or shape a script that speaks

31

the language of cinema. Describing locations, writing out dialogue and detailing the action is only a part of what is required to make a well-written screenplay. From there you must arrange that information into a visual script that communicates in the language of film. Otherwise, it's just words on paper or stage direction for a teleplay.

So let's take a look at two different samples.

SAMPLE A

SAMPLE A SCRIPT

FADE IN:

EXT. DARK ALLEY – NIGHT

RHETT WILEY, thirty something steps into a long dark alley. Garbage cans and trash fill the wet and soggy asphalt. A red neon sign with the letters "RAT'S NEST" flickers above Rhett's head. He is wearing a black coat with a white fedora tilted over his blue eyes.

He steps forward and looks down at the ground. We see, JACK CAMPTON. Jack is laying on his side holding what looks to be his stomach. There is a puddle of blood underneath him. He squints up at the neon sign and sighs.

                    JACK
          You finally got to me Wiley. You
          finally got to me.

Rhett steps back and places a small hand gun into his pocket.

                    RHETT
          Well, you deserve it. Making me fly
          to all of those cities. You have
          any idea how expensive air travel
          is?

Jack laughs and looks down, coughing up his laugh.

                    JACK
          Yeah. I guess you're right.

Rhett looks away for a second.

                    JACK (CONT'D)
          Well finish the job.

                    RHETT
          Na. I think I'll let them do it.

Jack's attention moves past Rhett to the end of the alley. Standing in the shadows lurks a bunch of staggering, and snarling zombies. Jack looks back to Rhett.

                    RHETT (CONT'D)
          This is for what you did to my
          car...

Rhett walks past Jack as he lays on the ground. Panic starts to consume the man.

Not awful, but kind of meh. Sample A depicts a scene where the writer is leaving out the majority of verbs and instead focuses on nouns that describe the setting. Let's see how Sample B does. It's the same scene, just laid out a little differently.

SAMPLE B

SAMPLE B SCRIPT

FADE IN:

EXT. DARK ALLEY - NIGHT

A red neon sign can be seen flickering in a puddle of murky water as it cuts out from an old brick wall.

The clicking of footsteps.

The silhouette of RHETT WILEY stands in the middle of a filthy inner city alleyway. The man looks up toward a streetlight, exposing his striking blue eyes, from under the rim of his tilted white fedora.

Then the sounds of painful grunting can be heard gently nearby. Rhett looks toward the ground and steps forward.

The face of a sweaty and painful face of JACK CAMPTON fills the frame. The man's focus lowers from the alleyway, and scans down to his waste area. His entire shirt is soaked with crimson. The man's agonizing face lifts back up to the alleyway before him.

                    JACK
          You finally got to me Wiley. You
          finally got to me.

Rhett steps back and places a small hand gun into his pocket.

                    RHETT
          Well, you deserve it. Making me fly
          to all of those cities. You have
          any idea how expensive air travel
          is?

Jack laughs and looks down again, coughing up most of his laugh.

                    JACK
          Yeah. I guess you're right.

Rhett looks away for a second, his eyes glimmering in and out of the shadows.

                    JACK (CONT'D)
          Well finish the job.

                    RHETT
          Na. I think I'll let them do it.

35

```
                                                       2.

        Jack's face goes white. The sounds of snarling creatures can
        be heard in the distance, reverberating steadily back down
        the alleyway. Moving around Rhett, we notice a pack of
        staggering zombies, tripping their way toward the men. Jack
        looks back to Rhett in horror.

                              RHETT (CONT'D)
                    This is for what you did to my
                    car...

        Jack's distraught face tracks Rhett as he passes. The sounds
        of Rhett's footsteps slowly dissipate with the approaching
        zombies.



        -- FIN --
```

Notice a difference? Which one spoke to you more as a reader? Did one feel faster/slower than the other? Personally, I like Sample B. Sample B offers a look at crafting your script in a more visual-cinematic expression. Whereas Sample A, despite being very thoughtful of setting and space, is focused on art direction. Sample A's style of writing is common among novice screenwriters and can lead to very boring reads overall. It lacks the ability to communicate from the audience's perspective, which in many ways, hinders your ability to create a pace-orientated movie.

Sample B's style, on the other hand, offers the reader a shot-for-shot account of the action, much like you would experience watching the actual movie. Sample B achieved this without doing the director of photography's or the director's jobs. It allows the reader to experience the film in real time as opposed to making assumptions as you would reading a novel.

This writing technique has changed my entire outlook on screenplay development. It has helped me identify the stronger screenplays versus the weaker ones. It has also helped convey ideas to my creative team more efficiently. Because I write and direct all of my own material, it is crucial to save the guesswork for my crew. This has allowed them to help me much better on the set. When you are making a micro-budget movie, eliminating the guesswork is invaluable.

A script with a limited number of locations and production headaches

There are many examples of successful movies that have been in limited-location settings. Take for example the movie *Last Shift*, directed by Anthony Diblasi, where the entire movie took place in a recently closed police precinct. Or, *All Is Lost*, directed by J. C. Chandor, starring Robert Redford, where he was lost at sea. The entire movie took place on a boat. You can also look at Rodrigo Cortes's 2010 hit, *Buried*, where a truck driver (Ryan Reynolds) finds himself stuck in a pine box somewhere in Iraq. Limited locations are your best friend when making a low-budget movie.

The real trick is to find a location that offers context to the story and multiple looks for your screenplay. But more importantly, look for script locations that do not require a ton of company moves, where your crew, cast, and equipment have to be physically packed up and transported. I have seen this so many times with young filmmakers, where they write in several location changes within the first twenty pages and plan for multiple company moves. They make the disastrous assumption that it will be easy to hop around to get the shots they need. In most cases they either fail to make their day, go way over budget, or get sloppy.

A few examples of locations that offer various settings are:

Shopping malls (parking-lot structures, restrooms, shops, boiler rooms.)

Office Buildings (restrooms, offices, parking structures, elevators, storage rooms.)

Mansions or large homes (kitchens, staff quarters, hallways, yards, pools, living quarters, garages, basements, offices, pools, gardens, forests, beaches, mountains.)

You also want to consider sound when writing for locations. Could your location produce loud crowd noises, road and air-traffic hindrances? Can the location be closed off for filming for a reasonable price? For example, closing off an airport terminal can cost thousands of dollars.

Try writing for locations that can be controlled for both sound purposes and logistical reasons. The less production fuss you have dealing with a location, the more you're able to shoot and less time servicing the fuss. Location is very important to your story, but it should not be a headache on top of all the other challenges you face making a movie.

It may also be wise to consider writing for locations you know or already have access to. A few years ago, I made a movie that was located in a series of underground tunnels. The first time I shot there was magical. The tunnels were underground and built in the 1970s, so you can imagine, they looked really creepy and awesome.

Moreover, the tunnels gave us unmatchable production value for a movie that was less than $30,000 to make. It took me months to secure all the appropriate insurance and permitting needed to film at this old government facility, but it was worth it. Nonetheless, we made sure that we kept things nice and easy for the location, so in the event I needed a setting like that again, I had some options.

A year after that movie released, my distributor called and asked if I could make another movie similar to the one we had just released. It was obvious that we needed the old location back. After a few phone calls and some updated paperwork, we secured the location for the new movie. However, this time, I was able to write much better with the space in mind. By utilizing the same location, I maximized my settings and pulled off the unimaginable task of filming a sci-fi thriller in less than eighteen days.

A script or idea that fits one of the more popular genre molds: action, suspense thriller, horror, sci-fi, children

This is a topic that I could spend an entire book on. Picking the right genre is the starting point to all positive and negative outcomes to a film production.

Before a movie is *greenlit* in Hollywood, it goes through several stages of what the industry calls *development*. This is a vetting process of economics and market research. There are teams of people who are employed to vet content. So my question to the reader is, *"Why not employ these same steps to your project development?"*

Let's be clear though, I am not an advocate for any particular genre, nor do I assume the role of expert on any particular one either. However, I do understand the market pretty well. My twenty-plus years in the movie industry has taught me a lot about what types of movies to make.

I would also like to stress that choosing a particular genre does not guarantee market success. Nonetheless, it can minimize the risk factor for your investment overall. There is a certain level of importance in operating within a set of market expectations, especially when making a micro-budget movie. The main reason is that certain categories are

42

more palatable for buyers. Additionally, some genres do not always require big stars or recognizable talent in order to be sold. Some genres can be sold in various territories across the world and speak a universal language. Let's take a look at the usual genre suspects.

Comedy: Huge risk

I love comedy. In fact, it is the genre I love to produce the most. I believe I am good at it. The most critically successful feature I have ever made was a comedy. Nonetheless, comedies are a micro-budget movie distributor's kryptonite! They are nearly impossible to sell overseas and require big names to help push them into relevancy with the fan base. Unless servicing some level of niche, or having an ensemble cast, comedies may even fall flat domestically. The sociology about comedy is that not everyone finds the same material funny. What Americans think is hilarious is typically dumb in the UK, and vice versa. People in Japan and other parts of Asia do not always laugh at the same things we do in America. Comedies can be very limiting to distributors and are typically passed on by most companies.

Comedies are about trust with the audience. In order for an viewer to laugh at something, there needs to be two things: trust in the character they are watching, and relatability. Most indie comedies that do not feature recognizable talent run the risk of distrust with their audience. If you are not familiar with the actor or actress who is doing the *funny*, then oftentimes it comes off as too campy or irritating. We mostly laugh at people we know, or at least relate to. If the character looks like someone you know or is in a situation that is familiar to you, then you may find the material funny. It takes time to establish this trust with an audience, time that micro movies do not have. If you don't believe me, try watching any indie comedy with faces you don't recognize, and see if you enjoy them as much as you do with Kevin Hart or Tina Fey. Viewers are very selective of comedy without knowing they are doing it.

All of that said, there are a few genres that are easier for buyers and distributors to digest. These genres often come with a lower level of risk, because there is already an established set of audience behaviors that can be identified. Knowing these behaviors is helpful for marketing and product positioning. Let's take a look at a few popular genres for low-budget movies.

Action: Think Safety, Budget, International Focus

According to many of the sales agents I have spoken with over the last five years, action movies are profoundly popular internationally. The market shows that if done correctly, you can garner major release potential. Action is one of those bullet-proof genres that is usually a win for large and micro-distribution firms. Action films can be made cheaply and still turn sales numbers. Of course, the best action film is one that has big names in it, but the second best action film is one that follows a relatable hero on an impossible journey.

With your budget, you might need to focus on the second best.

That said, I advise against producing in this genre, unless they have at least a $150,000 budget or more. Doing this genre effectively takes a decent level of money and technical skills. Plus, action movies require a ton of production needs in order to execute them safely.

When dealing with action, it's important that you avoid crafting big action scenes that require explosions, lots of vehicle stunts, and/or any combat portrayal that involves many people, such as war reenactments. However, if you have the special visual effects and animation skills, then you might be able to hurdle over some of those limitations.

Here are a few themes that could help your action budget stay small, but keep things big.

1. **The standoff: Everyone goes to one place to kill each other.**

2. **The rescue: The hero goes looking to save their loved one in a place.**

3. **The escape: The hero must escape the location before the bad guys get back.**

4. **Revenge: The hero checks off a list of wrongdoers.**

5. **Pinned down: The elite group of soldiers is pinned down in a place, and one of them is the outlier.**

When taking on a new genre, I research contemporary movies that have done more with less. When I think of low-budget action movies, *El Mariachi,* directed by Robert Rodriguez ($7,000 USD) and *Bronson,* directed by Nicolas Winding Refn ($250,000 USD) come to mind. Each of these movies focused primarily on the main character's survival in the moment. Despite having some really intense scenes, these two movies kept things simple. They used clever editing and cinematography to "up" the tension and excitement.

Using tricks like hand-to-hand combat and gunfights is a way to keep the action high and the cost low. But I must stress, you have to do it well. Having a stunt choreographer and a DP who knows how to shoot action is crucial. Moreover, you want to make sure your actors are safe. I cannot stress this enough. It is advised to hire professional stunt people to perform any physical stunt. The last thing you want is to get anyone injured. Nonprofessional stunt work from regular cast and crew is very risky and jeopardizes your entire production. One mistake or miscalculation could shut down your entire production.

Your decision to make an action movie should depend mainly on how well you can do things safely. If the stunts can be tricked-out with the camera, then no sweat. You might be able to have an actor do their own punch, push, trip, kick, or even a simple fall. But for anything that requires serious actions not limited to weapons, rigging, vehicles, high falls, animal stunts, explosions, and projectiles—or anything that could seriously harm or kill a cast or crew person—hire a stunt professional.

Additionally, budget time and money into blocking out scenes before you shoot. Do not rush preproduction or take shortcuts with safety. With anything that requires an actor to trip, fall, or appear to take a punch, be sure they have the appropriate body protection. This could include knee and elbow pads, stomach protection, back braces, face protection, and/or something to protect their head. It's also wise if an actor is going to do his or her own small trip, slip, or fall to a knee to have some padding on the floor. Some actors are adamant about doing their own stunts. You want to have honest conversations with the actor and know his or her abilities. They should also understand the risk associated with the minor stunt. If they are not in the best physical shape or health, then even the smallest stunt could be a catastrophe.

It's important to take every precaution possible to protect your cast and crew on set. If you do not have the budget for safety, then you need to rethink the type of action movie you are trying to make. Maybe you can employ some digital tricks. Your safety preparation should match the level of action movie you are trying to make. If you have explosions, then it is essential to have a team of pyrotechnics experts who can safely execute those demands. Plus, you will need to have all the appropriate insurance and permits for your activity. If you can't afford real pyro, then find some way to do things digitally. Fake it in post!

Guns and weapons are also easy tools for action movies, but I would stress to make sure you are shooting scenes in secured areas, away from public view. If you have a public scene that involves guns or any other weapons, you must have the appropriate permits, security, and police presence to make sure your scene is not misinterpreted as an actual event. This includes filming in front of private residences, where the action can be seen from public roads or other houses. Moreover, you should always have a weapons handler and expert on set for these scenes.

A few years ago, there was a crew filming a music video in the parking lot of a gas station. The scene involved a fake carjacking. The filmmakers did not have permits to shoot, and the police responded after someone noticed the commotion. The police ended up shooting one of the filmmakers. Luckily the filmmaker survived, but you get the moral of the story!

With action movies, the bottom line is safety. Injuries on any movie set is a concern, but with action movies, you are increasing the risk of trouble simply because of stunts and weapons.

The punch line for making an action movie is "keep things simple." Consider having the entire movie take place in one location, such as a warehouse, a tunnel, or a forest. Wherever it is, it should allow you to focus more on the action than on moving crew and people around.

Sci-Fi: Think type of sci-fi, technical team needed, locations, and visual effects

The genre of science fiction can not be addressed in a few paragraphs. However, I want to point out some of the basics to consider when you are producing this genre. The phrase *economy of scale* comes to mind when I think about sci-fi. Science fiction comes in all shapes and sizes. Never assume that one style of sci-fi is relatable to all people across the genre landscape. For example, the 2014 hit, *El Machina*, directed by Alex Garland, is a different sci-fi breed from Marvel's *Guardians of the Galaxy*. M. Night Shyamalan's *Signs* and Ridley Scott's *Alien* are different beasts. When working in science fiction, I always assume that I will disappoint fans to some extent. The genre bar is so high for science fiction that it's nearly impossible to make a movie that pleases everyone. Even George Lucas and Ridley Scott have taken criticism from fans over the years.

Sci-fi fans are also among the most vocally critical base that the movie industry has. Scoring any level of audience approval is somewhat a crapshoot. I discovered this firsthand with my movie, *Alien Domicile*. Even though my numbers and sales were fantastic, the alien fan base devoured me online. If you have thin skin, or do not like people criticizing you, sci-fi is the worst place to start. But if you are like me, negative criticism is a positive motivator in my creative endeavors.

Here are a few basic themes that could help you keep things small and still effective.

1. Trapped in a robot box.

2. Aliens are hunting the heroes.

3. Marooned in a strange place.

4. Various memories and perspectives.

5. Human experimentation gone wild and wrong.

6. **Human mutation gone well, then not so well.**

7. **Time travel (people travel to this time, so you can save money).**

8. **Parallel dimensions (apples are purple in this dimension).**

9. **Super abilities, like moving things with your mind or seeing the future.**

When developing science fiction, I first figure out what type of story has the best audience potential. I also consider what's currently popular and do a little research to see what's coming next. If I am making a movie about an alien, I like to consider the elements that are within that type of specific sci-fi genre. What type of alien? Are they the aggressors or the lovers. Are the humans the bad guys? What do people expect? I also look at films that are similar in scope, and study what worked and what didn't. From that point on, I can borrow themes and gags that service my own plot.

You can make a sci-fi work on a budget, but costs can escalate fast if you are not careful. Due to the nature of this genre, you are inventing props and creating environments that are not common in our world. This is why I like making science fiction that involves supernatural powers in contemporary settings. I try to place my characters in unnatural situations while keeping the story grounded in reality. I avoid subjects such as robots, modern civilizations, drone armies, spaceships, and epic space battles.

Regardless of what your movie involves, try to understand your limitations and work within them as best as you can. Sometimes you cannot afford to show the entire spaceship, but you might be able to make an outstanding bridge in your buddy's garage. The other way you can keep your cost low is to find a location that looks unnatural, whether it's a strange desert or an exotic city landscape. Finding a place that looks *out of this world* can save you tons of money and give your flick a bigger-budget appearance.

I don't even think of production until I lock down my locations. Location is everything. It not only serves as the backdrop, but becomes a character in the story Do not be afraid to rework ideas to make them fit within your budget parameters and available locations. I think of movies like *Primer,* directed by Shane Carruth, or Vincenzo Natali's *Cube* as great examples of this. These movies turned indie sci-fi on its head, not because of technical wizardry or exotic locations, but by making their small locations service the narrative. These filmmakers worked within their economy of scale to make cult classics with very little capital.

Lastly, for this summary on science fiction, I would suggest you build a visual-effects team now. Do not wait until postproduction to figure this out. There are so many great digital artists looking for work. Most of them are straight out of college. Try to find people who share your passion and can work with you on your budget. Use social media to your benefit and create an online presence that attracts creativity. If you build a competent team now, you will make your development process much easier. You will discover what you can achieve, and find ways to work around limitations. The other alternative is to learn visual effects yourself. Luckily, we can find great educational videos on YouTube.

Horror: Think practical effects, playing with dark spaces, and common themes.

Scares are cheap. They also don't require star power. Fear is an international language. It doesn't require a lot of backstory or baggage to execute. However, you will need to make sure you have all the elements of the genre to ensure you don't disappoint die-hard fans. Horror movies are great for low-budget filmmakers, because they typically call for singular locations that oftentimes trap the characters in one setting. This works great for your production schedule.

Here are a few other themes that seem to work well in this genre:

1. Escaping the killer.

2. Hiding from the monster.

3. Vengeful ghost in the closet.

4. People eating people is normal here.

5. Witches who hate everyone.

6. Creatures that live in neighborhoods.

Another great thing about horror is that with a reasonable amount of effort, even a novice can pull off some visual effects practically. Unlike sci-fi, horror movies can be a little more forgiving on the low-budget scale. The only warning here is to make sure you consult with a distributor, or at least do some basic investigation prior to locking things in. There may be very particular subgenres in horror that do not sell as well as others. It's always wise to consult with the people who have to sell this stuff. Moreover, if the gore and violence is too heavy, it may not appeal to international buyers or allow the movie to be sold in some retail stores and video-on-demand (VOD) platforms. If you are trying to do a horror film that will sell, try keeping your movie within mainstream limits. Disturbing is one thing, but the last thing you want is to make your content so distasteful that it cannot even be uploaded on YouTube. I like staying in the creature or supernatural realm; these stories are universal and can appeal to broader audiences. Every culture can relate to ghosts and monsters phenomena. Plus, these types of horror films can also cross over into sci-fi, drama and thriller pretty easily.

Suspense Thriller: Think about setting the clock and mixing genres

Much like the genre of horror, suspense calls to a person's natural instincts. Tension and suspense is always a useful tool no matter what genre you are playing with. Thrillers can come in the form of a crime story, chase-action movie, sci-fi, and supernatural themes. By tapping into the natural emotions of the human experience, you can bypass language and cultural barriers to find better success in the international marketplace.

Thrillers hit a few basic notions of fear and stress.

1.　　**The fear of death.**

2.　　**The stress of being hunted.**

3.　　**The stress of hiding something from others.**

4.　　**The fear of the unknown.**

5.　　**The stress of a loved one being harmed.**

6.　　**The stress of hiding secrets.**

7.　　**The fear of the universe around them.**

This category cannot be added to this topic without mentioning Alfred Hitchcock, the master of thriller and suspense movies. I suggest watching classics like *Rear Window*, *Rope*, *Vertigo*, *The Birds,* and *Psycho*. Each of his films used the technique of creating impossible situations for their characters while letting the audience in on things that even the main character isn't aware of. This technique of *knowing what is unknown* is a perfect device to drive audiences crazy.

Another great tool of thriller movies is when the *clock is set*. Once the clock has been set, the tension is ratcheted up each and every second the movie passes. It's a cheap tool for you as a filmmaker. Here are a few ways you could use the clock.

1. **The escape must happen before the bad guys return.**

2. **The last train is leaving in two hours.**

3. **The killer is losing her patience.**

4. **The virus is winding down into its final deadly chapter.**

5. **The killer boyfriend is coming home soon.**

These tools can offer your subplot a huge boost. I always suggest adding some level of urgency to any film, regardless of genre. This keeps the audience on the edge of their seats, while the main storyline ticks along. Also, by adding the clock, and allowing the audience to know things that are unknown to the characters, that will take the tension level up tenfold.

Here's an example:

We know the killer is in the room, but the heroine doesn't know. She enters anyway.

Children and Family Films: Think, production value, morals, and television

This genre of movies is highly overlooked by aspiring filmmakers. Nonetheless, the demand for good-quality family movies is currently increasing. If you can shoot a well-produced family driven movie, you might discover a world of commercial possibilities. Plus, the competition level is low. Obviously, companies like Disney have the market cornered at the studio level, but with the rise of VOD, film buyers are looking at filling their libraries with more family tonnage without the Disney price tag.

Although family movies have to be done right, there is a strict set of guidelines that companies follow. Just because you have a talking dog or a puppet, it doesn't automatically qualify it as a family movie. These movies are typically set within the framework of classic family entertainment. Themes and storylines should be simple to follow, and plots should move fast. Nudity, sex, drugs, alcohol, weapons, and extreme violence is avoided in this genre at all costs.

Before diving in, you should determine which type of family movie you want to make.

Here are a few directions in the genre that you can consider:

1. **Holiday movies**

2. **Animals**

3.   **Kids rule the world**

4.   **Kids' adventure**

5.   **Animation for young children**

6.   **Prekindergarten (educational)**

7.   **Magic and wizardry**

8.   **Games and technology**

Faith-Based and Religious Movies

There is an ever-increasing demand for faith-based and religious programming. Much like the family genre, this category is lower on the competitive scale. This genre is very specific, and can, in some cases, offer you more unique financing options from organizations, faith groups, religious institutions, local parishes, and normal parishioners that are not normally available to other categories of films. These movies also come with built-in audiences that can support your production from the development stage into distribution.

As we look at the faith-based genre, I should also note, these types of movies have a ton of ancillary value, including workbooks, novels, workshops, merchandise, and special-event screenings. Faith-based movies could be an incredible genre for any inspired producer to tackle. This genre is in need of new ideas and voices.

Here are a few themes that can service this genre:

1. **Lost faith; need to find it.**

2. **Spreading the dogma.**

3. **Doing the right thing against the odds.**

4. **A mission from the heavens.**

5. **Holiday movies with a religious context.**

The most important thing about faith movies is that, not only does the script have to be tight and squeaky clean, but it should also follow the dogma of its cause. If you are making a Christian film, then those beats should reflect the teachings of the bible. This is why many faith-based movies have workbooks, or pamphlets accompanied with the film at public screenings. The heroes and heroines should also reflect the values of the faith and play by the rules. The only disadvantage to this genre is that the story has to walk a particular fine line and has to be leery of alienating or offending its audience. Subjects like sex, violence, or occult material may be too offensive to this audience and should be carefully calculated before considering its use.

A screenplay with a limited cast count

Cast matters. A small cast matters more. In recent years I have worked hard at developing stories that require a very small cast. My recent movies typically involve three to five actors and rarely exceed ten people. When making a micro-budget movie, consolidation is key. Too many performers can drive up labor costs and inhibit your ability to stay on budget. Keeping your cast size smaller forces you to do more with less and places the priority on performance, more so than scale.

Movies that have large ensembles are very difficult to manage even at a big budget level. If you are making a movie with five actors or fewer, you should be able to make a $30,000–$50,000 micro-budget movie. On average, you should expect to have your cast on set anywhere from ten to fifteen days. This is minding that your script is between seventy-five and ninety pages. If you have more cast members, your daily talent cost will escalate.

Now you may be asking, "what if the actors are doing the movie for free, or for copy and credit?" And to that, I would still suggest you keep your numbers low. Let's explore a few points.

Fewer mouths to feed:

The more folks you have on set, the more mouths you need to feed. Now this may sound trivial, but it adds up; every sandwich counts.

Insurance costs may rise. If your cast and crew numbers are large, your general liability and workers'-compensation insurance policies may be higher too.

You still need to pay your talent something:

Whether it's deferments, gas money, or just screeners to the completed film, keeping your post-obligations will make your life happy.

*(A special note here: I don't recommend not paying your talent. Pay them some money, whether it's a flat fee or daily rate. It may not need to be Screen Actors Guild (SAG) scale, but it should make it worth the actors' time. This makes for good relationships and places a professionalism on set that you can't create without compensation.)

A project you can self-produce and finance between $30k and $50k

The most common question I get when I talk about the $30k–$40k budget model is "What do you get for $30K?" To answer that questions, there needs to be a few points of understanding. But in short, the answer always is "It depends on what skills and tools you already have at your disposal."

The quality of film you produce should not be reflected in your budget constraints. In fact it's the other way around.

Your script should reflect two things:

1. Your abilities as a moviemaker

2. A production that can be shot in 15–18 days or fewer, with limited locations and cast.

Regardless if you're a seasoned filmmaker with several movies under your wings, or you're just getting started, you should know and understand your abilities and use them to your advantage. Any person can make a good movie as long as their limitations are worked into the equation.

For example, I am not a guru when it comes to computer animation and digital effects. Therefore, when developing my movies, I look to simplify those areas and make them more palatable for my budget and skill set. If a scene requires some level of post effects, I carefully deliberate that and try to either find ways of doing the effects practical (without needing to hire a computer animator), or I simply try to shoot around the issue and allow the audience to use their imaginations. In either case the solution should represent the best possible outcome for the story and movie experience. This shouldn't be confused with the notion of cutting corners or doing less. This simply means the idea of working within your parameters to achieve a favorable outcome that satisfies both the audiences' expectations and your budgetary constraints.

Now that being said, there are some creators who excel in visual effects, and therefore are able to maximize their production value with their natural skills. They understand how to do those things, which in turn saves them buckets money. They can also expand on things that perhaps a moviemaker like myself wouldn't be able to do. It may also offer them more latitude in the types of genres they can tackle and worlds they can create.

You may also have access to an extraordinary location, expensive props, machinery, special film equipment, or other valuable things that would normally cost most of us a lot of money. By having those things, you can also expand your production value without having to weigh down your budget. I've used this to my advantage to compensate for other areas in my budget limitations. I have a ton of amazing resources and connections, and I use them to their fullest when needing to maximize my production value. So, I hope you see that by evaluating the things you have in your toolbox can help you maximize effectiveness in the type of movie you're trying to make, because at the end of the day, a majority of your money should go to talent, food, crew, and insurance. Develop within your strengths!

A script with the page count between 75 and 80 pages

I'm sure you've heard the adage *a script should be as long as it needs to be.* And as much as I could agree with that statement, the producer side of my brain kicks in and says, "That's fine as long as it's not more than eighty pages!" It is truly astounding to me when first-time moviemakers set out to make movie scripts that are around 120 pages, and in some cases even more For every page you have, you need to factor in time to shoot it.

On average, you can expect to film four to six pages per day. That is taking into accounts that your talent is ready to go and all cylinders are firing like they should. I truly believe that even the best filmmakers would struggle to get a meaningful six pages per day filmed without utterly rushing it. So let's be conservative and play with some basic math and add a two-day contingency just for safety.

*80 **Page Script*** / 5 pages per day + 2 days of contingency = **18 days**

*75 **Page Script*** / 5 pages per day + 2 days of contingency = **17 days**

*72 **Page Script*** / 5 pages per day + 2 days of contingency = **16.4 days**

Even at seventy-two pages, you can still make a movie that qualifies for a feature-length status. I try to keep my scripts under eighty pages. This allows me to film more comfortably throughout my schedule and still have time to breathe for pickup shots and postprinciple photography needs.

The other issue I'd like to outline is that screenplays that are laced with dialogue can also be a slow-down factor when you're shooting. Not only will it require patience for your actors, it will also make you vulnerable to sound issues and other production hassles that are most certain to happen.

I remember shooting a scene that was nearly four pages of people talking around the table, scheming a heist that was about to happen. The scene had several actors, and despite only being four pages of dialogue, it took us two days to film just that scene. We had everything from actors forgetting their lines and getting flustered, to dogs barking, and airplanes ruining perfectly good takes. It was at that moment, I decided to start making silent movies with occasional talking.

Knowing where to start

Here's the thing. If you don't know where to start in finding a screenplay that hits these areas that I've mentioned, do not fret. There are tons of great examples of movies out there that are certain to give you some inspiration. Do a search for movies (successful movies) that were successful in the criteria mentioned in this chapter. Take the time to reverse engineer what others did, and learn from it.

CHAPTER 4
The Art of the Breakdown

There is no more important aspect of preproduction than the breakdown. The breakdown is a systematic and thorough evaluation of your screenplay. It allows you the time to not only understand the components needed to make your film, but it also allows you to budget, schedule, and craft a plan for completing your project. However, my process of breaking down a script may be fundamentally different than most assistant directors and line-producers. Other than exporting an initial scene report from my screenplay program, I break my scripts down the old-fashioned way, scene by scene, and then arrange my data into a simple and easy-to-read flow chart that ultimately becomes the master-production schedule.

One of the biggest aspects of the breakdown process is to understand your movie inside and out and the ability to see your entire production at a glance. This may seem obvious, but it couldn't be any more important for a filmmaker to visualize his or her battle plan before entering principle photography. You should be able to glance at a report, whether on paper or digital, and know how many scenes you have in each location, how many pages per location, what actors are needed on each day, what props and specialty equipment is needed for every single scene, and how many pages you can shoot in a day. Moreover, because most films are not shot in the order of the script, seeing your production plan fast and easy is even more important for continuity. This holds true even if you're the writer of your own script, but especially if you are not. You need to dissect each scene and know in a flash what each day of production calls for.

Do your breakdown manually

In today's age we're always looking for an easy button. Time is everything these days, and it seems we never have enough of it. Instant gratification feels good in the moment, but when it comes to preproduction, rushing or taking short cuts will cost you big time. I do not use breakdown software to complete my process. Now this may seem archaic to some, considering there are amazing programs that can do the job fast, efficiently, and relatively well. However, using programs to breakdown your script robs you of the creative process of designing your production from the ground up. Moreover, the reports that are generated by some of these programs (although very thorough) can be very complicated to read quickly and seem like Martian manuscripts to cast and crew.

That said, I'm not saying breakdown programs do not serve their purpose. Programs are wonderful for breaking down larger productions where you have assistant directors and line-producers who can help you

78

manage things from a far. But when making a small movie like the one we are aiming for in this book, knowing everything allows you to make fast decisions when things go awry (and they will go awry) and helps you keep the train on the tracks. I will show you, not only how to break your script into tangible components to film, but how to create a clean and simple chart that a fifth grader could manage.

There are seven basic steps to breaking down your script:

Locations: Breaking each scene into locations and physical places.

Cast: Knowing what cast members are needed for each scene and day of filming.

Props & Specialty Equipment: An itemized list all of the props and special equipment needed for each scene and each day they are needed. This includes cool film toys, such as drones, car mounts, stabilizing systems, and so on.

Description: An easy-to-remember description of each scene. VERY IMPORTANT! Something that even if you hadn't read the screenplay, you would know what the scene is about and what is happening. Moreover, any clues to what happened in the previous scene could also be helpful.

Page count: Page count for each scene, accompanied by page and scene numbers.

Organizing: Arranging all of this data into categories from like-minded locations to cast frequency.

Scheduling: Dividing up the categories into actual shooting days.

Before we start, let me mention that it takes me an average of two to three weeks to do a proper breakdown of a script ranging from 75 to 90 pages. I do it in phases. Each phase is reviewed and cross-checked with the script to ensure accuracy. So let me begin with my step-by-step overview of my particular process.

PHASE ONE:

After I complete a screenplay, I use a program called Final Draft to export what is called a *scene report*. Note: Most screenwriting programs have this ability in one fashion or another. If you don't have an option for this with your program, or if you're using a word-processing program, you can, of course, do this phase manually. Having a scene-report option just allows you to save a little time by starting your initial breakdown phase.

WHERE TO LOOK

In Final Draft 10, the Scene-Report option is located under Tools>Reports>Scene Report.

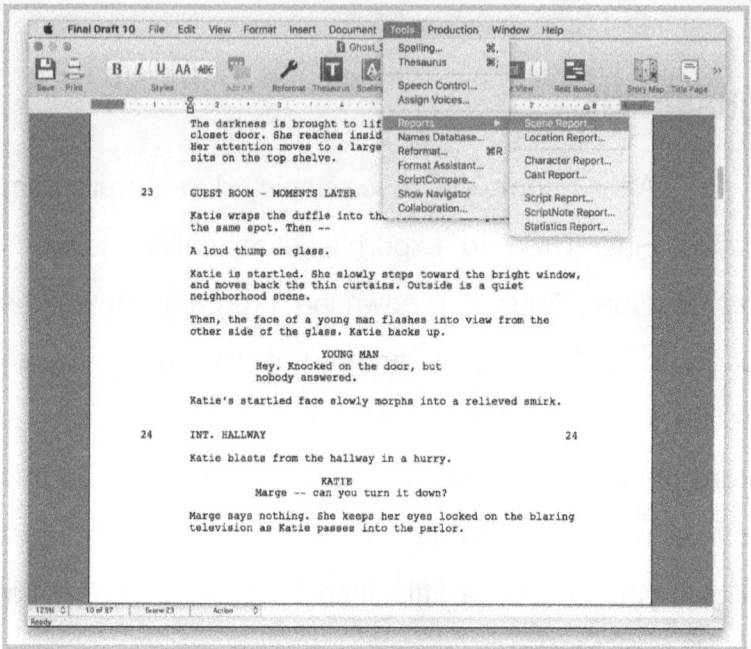

You can run the report and list your scenes based by alphabetical order, page count, script order, location, scene order, longest scene, and so on. I usually like to run reports in script order. This helps me follow along with the script as I go through the initial process.

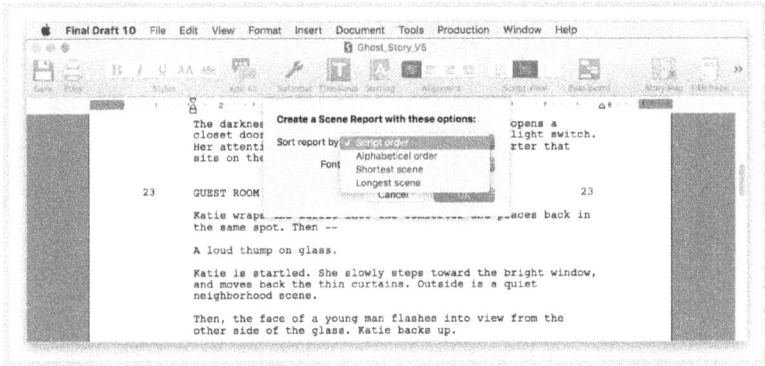

WHAT A REPORT LOOKS LIKE

This example is what the report looks like after the program is finished.

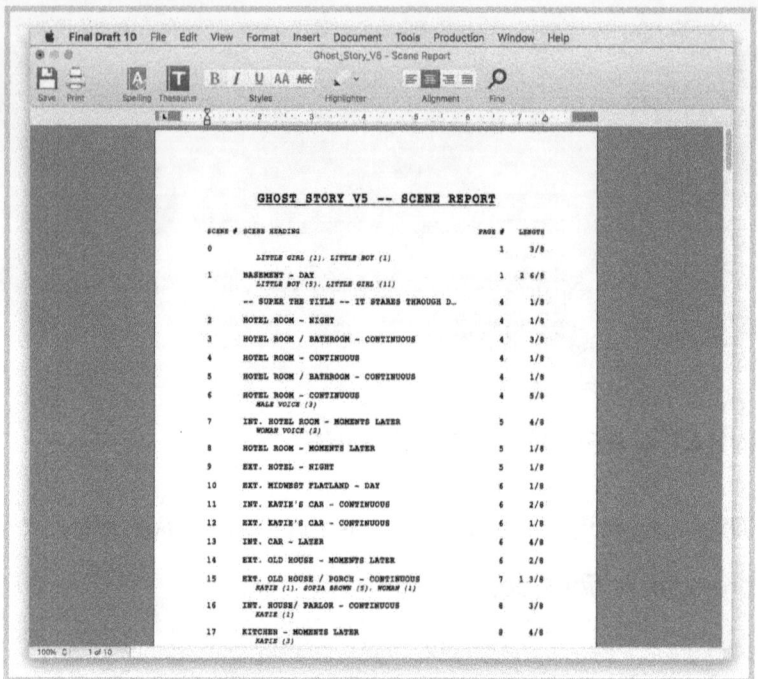

Once I get this report, I actually go back in, read the screenplay, and attribute the particulars of a scene to each of those little scene-report areas. It's also important to note that with the reports you generate from most programs like Final Draft 10, you can type directly into the scene report and modify things right away. You can copy and paste things around, as well as create subheadings and make your breakdown look really pretty.

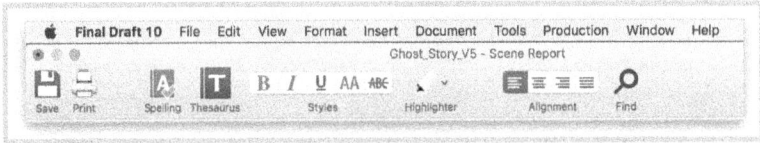

In Final Draft 10, you have many of the editing tools that most word-processing software offers.

BEFORE

What the program gives you from the scene report.

AFTER

```
   Scene Heading                              Page #  Length


   1 BASEMENT - DAY                              1     3.25
   Players: LITTLE BOY (Brian), LITTLE GIRL (Katie), Ghost
   Description: First scene of the movie! Little Katie and Brian
   venture into the basement.
   Props: Vintage photo of girls, Mask, Old Trunk, Flashlight,
   Lightbulb
   Stunts: Tripping on steps, minor falls and jumps
   Special Equipment: N/A
   VEFX: N/A
```

After I get done with it!

From there, I am able to put in the cast that's going to be in these scenes, as well as the props, stunts, special effects, and even visual effects. Most importantly, I add a simple scene description that could help even below-the-line crew know what's going on.

Note that this part of the process takes the longest, because it requires you to read through the script and make a diagnostic report on each scene.

This is a tedious task, and one that shouldn't be rushed. Allow for at least two weeks to do this phase.

PHASE TWO

From there, I arrange everything based on location or physical place where I could film. I do this by copying and pasting location areas next to each other in the report. Just be sure to delete the ones you copy, paste, and move elsewhere in the report, so you don't have duplicate scenes.

In this example, I copied and pasted all of the "Brian's Apartment Scenes" together.

```
------------------------- DAY 11 (2.50 PAGES) -----------------------------------
96 INT. BRIAN'S APARTMENT / KITCHEN - LATER                        44      .25
Players: BRIAN
Description: Brian arrives home and heads for the refrigerator.
Props: wallet, car keys, beer
Stunts: N/A
Special Equipment: N/A


97 BRIAN'S APARTMENT / LIVING ROOM - CONTINUOUS                    44      .25
Players: LOREN
Description: Loren waits up for Brian.
Props: Loren's cellphone, beer
Stunts: N/A
Special Equipment: N/A


98 BRIAN'S APARTMENT / KITCHEN - CONTINUOUS                        44      .125
Players: BRIAN
Description: Brian grabs a beer and slams the refrigerator door.
Props: beer
Stunts: N/A
Special Equipment: N/A


99 INT. BRIAN'S APARTMENT / LIVING ROOM - CONTINUOUS               44      .125
Players: BRIAN, LOREN
Description: Brian walks past Loren, ignoring her.
Props: Loren's cellphone, beer
Stunts: N/A
Special Equipment: N/A
```

SCENE HEADING	PAGE #	LENGTH

100 BRIAN'S APARTMENT / HOME OFFICE - CONTINUOUS   44   .75
Players: BRIAN, LOREN
Description: Brian jumps on his laptop. Loren follows him and stands at the
threshold.
Props: beer, laptop, desk clutter, swivel desk chair
Stunts: N/A
Special Equipment: N/A

127 INT. BRIAN'S APARTMENT / BEDROOM - CONTINUOUS   63   .25
Players: BRIAN, LOREN
Description: Brian can't sleep. He gets out of bed, leaving Loren asleep.
Props: N/A
Stunts: N/A
Special Equipment: Jib, or camera to be mounted over the bed

If I have scenes that take place in an office hallway and other scenes that call for an office lobby, I could group all of these similar setting locations into a clump.

In this sample, notice I lumped interior car scenes into the exterior scenes of an old house. The reason for this is because the car scenes take place outside the house. I could theoretically film those shots the same day or time frame as I do these exteriors.

EXTERIOR HOUSE LOCATIONS (16.25 PAGES)

-------------------------- DAY 5 *(6 PAGES)* --------------------------

136 INT. CAR - CONTINUOUS   66   .25

Players: KATIE, BASEBALL BOY

Description: Katie jumps into car. A baseball slams into the driver's side window. She sees a little boy running off. She the gets a text from Brian.

Props: duffle, cellphone with the text: FOUND SOMETHING. CAN WE MEET?

Stunts: N/A

Special Equipment: N/A

14 EXT. OLD HOUSE (YARD) - MOMENTS LATER   6   .25

Players: KATIE

Description: Katie walks toward the house, taking notice of the old house.

Props: duffle, Katie's cell phone, bag of groceries

Stunts: N/A

Special Equipment: Ronin/ Gimbal

VEFX: N/A

SCENE HEADING	PAGE #	LENGTH

15 EXT. OLD HOUSE / PORCH - CONTINUOUS   7   1 .125
Players: KATIE, SOFIA BROWN
Description: Katie knocks on door. No answer, then Sofia Brown exits.
Conversation about taking care of Marge.
Props: duffle, Katie's cell phone, bag of groceries, Sofia's business card
Stunts: N/A
Special Equipment: N/A
VEFX: N/A

13 INT. CAR - LATER   6   .50
Players: KATIE, WALTER
Description: Katie wakes up in the neighborhood and sees old man with
groceries.
Props: Katie's Car, duffle, Katie's cell phone, bag of groceries
Stunts: N/A
Special Equipment: N/A
VEFX: N/A

48 EXT. HOUSE / PORCH - CONTINUOUS   19   1 .25
Players: KATIE, WALTER
Description: Katie returns to the front door and gives it another solid
knock. She bumps into the old man as he brings more groceries.
Props: Bag of groceries
Stunts: N/A
Special Equipment: N/A

Arranging your breakdown like this is crucial. Ideally, when you go to a location, you don't want to set up your equipment and then have to move it somewhere else. So, if you're filming interiors at, let's say a church or a school, you want to try to do everything you can at that location within the same

91

timeframe, whether it be all in one day or in a course of a week. That's very, very important.

The next aspect of phase two is seeing into the future and anticipating cast scheduling. This can be done regardless if you have your actors or not. The main goal of this exercise is to think about their time on set. Arranging each location in order of cast frequency is the start to crafting an efficient and budget-conscious schedule. One of the biggest mistakes most indie filmmakers make is that they do not utilize cast time correctly.

For example, a call sheet calls for JOAN to be on set at 8:00 a.m., but she ends up not even filming until 2:00 p.m. Or, you have JOHN come to set for two out of five of his scenes with JOAN, and then have him come back two days later to film other scenes with JOAN at the same location. Doing things this way will not only require you to pay JOHN for his extra days on set, but may cause you to waste JOAN's time, and she's not going to be happy about that. But the biggest thing to watch out for is time waste. If you have JOHN at 8:00 a.m., try to film all of his scenes in order and get him wrapped as soon as you can. An example of poor cast scheduling will have JOHN film one scene, then stand down for five hours while shooting other scenes, when JOHN's scenes could have just been knocked out in order. Now, obviously if you need JOHN for one scene in the DAY and one at NIGHT, this isn't avoidable, but do your best to think through these items as you start to arrange the scene locations in actual shooting order.

In this sample, I arranged the location scenes so that way I could film all of Roger's scenes in order, then Amelia and the Dead Security Guard. Now you will notice that I have Katie stand down for one scene, and that's because it's only a short scene. Maybe she could break while I do the other quick scene. I'd rather wrap up the three other actors first, because it leaves fewer people lingering on set.

```
------------------------- DAY 19 (7.125 PAGES) ----------------------------
197 INT. PARLOR - CONTINUOUS                                  83      .25
Players: ROGER, KATIE
Description: Katie leads Roger into the hallway.
Props: gun
Stunts: N/A
Special Equipment: N/A


198 INT. HALLWAY - CONTINUOUS                                 83      .25
Players: ROGER, KATIE
Description: Roger backs Katie through the hallway, past the closed basement

door and into her guest room. The basement door handle slowly turns.
Props: gun
Stunts: N/A
Special Equipment: N/A
```

SCENE HEADING	PAGE #	LENGTH
<u>200 INT. HALLWAY - CONTINUOUS</u>	85	.25
Players: ROGER		
Description: Amelia drags Roger into the basement.		
Props: gun		
Stunts: N/A		
Special Equipment: N/A		
<u>199 INT. GUEST ROOM - CONTINUOUS</u>	83	2
Players: ROGER, KATIE, AMELIA		
Description: Katie leads Roger into the trap. Amelia attacks Roger.		
Props: gun, duffle		
Stunts: N/A		
Special Equipment: N/A		
<u>27 INT. GUEST ROOM - NIGHT</u>	13	.25
Players: KATIE, DEAD SECURITY GUARD		
Description: Katie can't sleep. Stares at the ceiling, then has the first dead Security Guard hallucination.		
Props: Guard uniform.		
Stunts: N/A		
Special Equipment: N/A		
VEFX: N/A		
<u>101 INT. HOUSE / GUEST ROOM - MORNING</u>	45	.25
Players: KATIE		
Description: Katie opens the curtains abruptly. She exits the room with determination.		
Props: curtains		
Stunts: N/A		
Special Equipment: N/A		

Time is the most valuable thing any living organism has. It's the one thing that can't be reimbursed or traded. Once it's gone, it's gone. Time efficiency is the most important aspect of indie filmmaking. You must work on this skill to run a production efficiently.

Another money-saving aspect of time management is that if you wrap people faster, the less likely you will need to feed and shelter them longer. Although it may feel cool to have an entourage of people hanging out on set, the more folks you have hanging around, the more mouths you'll need to feed, and feet to trip over. A lean set-place is your oasis. Don't get caught up in the entourage mentality. Wrap people and get them the hell off your set. This also goes for crew. Only have the crew you actually need. Don't overstaff your ranks with people who are not actually necessary to be there. Keep it LEAN...LEAN! LEAN!

Below you will see another example of how I arranged things so that I can maximize my cast frequency and save for the budget. Mind you, both of the characters, BRIAN and KATE, are in hallway scenes and guest-room scenes. But rather than having BRIAN come back a different day just to film that one scene in the guest room, I arranged it so he could wrap everything I needed with him in that hallway on that day.

SCENE HEADING	PAGE #	LENGTH
200 INT. HALLWAY - CONTINUOUS	85	.25
Players: ROGER		
Description: Amelia drags Roger into the basement.		
Props: gun		
Stunts: N/A		
Special Equipment: N/A		
199 INT. GUEST ROOM - CONTINUOUS	83	2
Players: ROGER, KATIE, AMELIA		
Description: Katie leads Roger into the trap. Amelia attacks Roger.		
Props: gun, duffle		
Stunts: N/A		
Special Equipment: N/A		
27 INT. GUEST ROOM - NIGHT	13	.25
Players: KATIE, DEAD SECURITY GUARD		
Description: Katie can't sleep. Stares at the ceiling, then has the first dead Security Guard hallucination.		
Props: Guard uniform.		
Stunts: N/A		
Special Equipment: N/A		
VEFX: N/A		
101 INT. HOUSE / GUEST ROOM - MORNING	45	.25
Players: KATIE		
Description: Katie opens the curtains abruptly. She exits the room with determination.		
Props: curtains		
Stunts: N/A		
Special Equipment: N/A		

```
41 HALLWAY - CONTINUOUS                                    17     .50
Players: KATIE, BRIAN
Description: Katie pivots back to the hallway after closing her guest room
door, to land face to face with Brian, who is wearing the mask.
Props: Mask
Stunts: N/A
Special Equipment: N/A
VEFX: N/A


43 HALLWAY - CONTINUOUS                                    18     .25
Players: KATIE, BRIAN
Description: Katie and Brain make their way back down the hallway after Katie
tosses the mask back into the basement.
Props: N/A
Stunts: N/A
Special Equipment: N/A
VEFX: N/A


63 HALLWAY - CONTINUOUS                                    24     .50
Players: BRIAN, KATIE
Description: Brian fixes the basement door with a new doorknob and lock, as
Katie watches, then asks him to fix the lightbulb.
Props: Electric screwdriver, tool bag, new doorknob, Coffees (x2), lightbulb
Stunts: N/A
Special Equipment: N/A


93 HALLWAY - CONTINUOUS                                    41     .50
Players: KATIE, BRIAN
Description: Katie gets anxious as she hears Brian rummaging in the basement.
He returns with Katie's duffle.
Props: duffle bag
Stunts: N/A
```

Now, I do understand that there will be some instances you will be required to call your cast back. This typically happens if you have too many pages to film in a particular location. However, if you are working with actors that you have brought in from out of town, you will need to put them into hotels and pay them per-diem for each day they are away (even if they are nonunion). To have an actor sitting around his or her hotel for a day is a waste of money. If it can be avoided, then avoid it. The moral of this story is consolidation. Consolidation is the key to success!

PHASE THREE

Walking the line

After you've arranged the script in order of location and cast frequency, now it's time to start walking the line and figuring out where to break the list into actual filming days. I like to approach the process by counting the page count of each cluster of locations and drawing my line around the five- to six-page mark, or in some cases even fewer, depending on what the scene requires. In some cases a quarter-page of script could be an entire week of filming. This is why knowing your scenes inside and out is very important.

In this sample, you'll notice I listed the total pages for the cluster of scenes, which here I am calling "Miscl Locations." There are a total of seventeen and a half pages in this cluster, but each separate day, I am only listing between one to three and a half pages per day.

MISCL LOCATIONS (17.5 PAGES)
--------------------------- DAY 9 (1.75 PAGES) ---------------------------

2-8 INT. HOTEL ROOM / BATHROOM - NIGHT	4-5	1.5

Players: KATIE

Description: We introduce Katie. She finishes up her bath to hear ex-boyfriend's voicemail, and the call from Sofia Brown with the State.

Props: Katie's Cellphone, duffle bag

Stunts: N/A

Special Equipment: N/A

VFX: N/A

9 EXT. HOTEL - NIGHT	5	.25

Players: KATIE

Description: Katie leaves hotel.

Props: Katie's Cellphone, duffle bag, Katie's Car

Stunts: N/A

```
SCENE HEADING                                    PAGE #   LENGTH

Special Equipment: Ronin/ Gimbal
VEFX: N/A


------------------------- DAY 10 (3.50 PAGES) -------------------------
124 INT. HOSPITAL RECORDS ARCHIVE - LATER             59      3 .50
Players: KATIE, BRIAN
Description: Katie and Brian rummage through old medical files. They discover
Amelia was the third daughter.
Props: various banker boxes of old medical files, Brian's I.D. Badge,
indexing labels "A-Z", Hoffman tab, Rolland Hoffman DD2-14, and medical
papers, Whitehall tab, ambulance report from the crash, old black and white
image Walter gave her,
Stunts: N/A
Special Equipment: N/A
------------------------- DAY 11 (2.50 PAGES) -------------------------
96 INT. BRIAN'S APARTMENT / KITCHEN - LATER           44        .25
Players: BRIAN
Description: Brian arrives home and heads for the refrigerator.
Props: wallet, car keys, beer
Stunts: N/A
Special Equipment: N/A
```

In the previous sample, you might look at that and ask why not film more locations since there's such a small page count per day. This may seem logical on paper. Of course, if I could consolidate three days on my schedule, I would. But in the example above, each of these locations are at complete separate places. Anytime you have to move your crew, cast, and

101

equipment (no matter how small), it's considered a "Company Move." More on this later.

The moral of this phase of the breakdown process is to not attempt to film more than six pages per day. I know what you're thinking: "It's super simple. I know exactly what I want!" or "The actors and crew won't mind filming for fifteen hours straight! Yippie!" In both of these ideologies, you fail to understand basic physics. One thing I can guarantee is that you will encounter time delays and production flubs, no matter how smart you think you are. This includes actors being overworked or having a bad day, which causes them to mess up lines or give you crumby performances, landscaping people or airplanes messing up your sound, something getting broken that needs to be replaced before the shot can go off, or just flat-out mutiny from your overworked crew. As I understand and respect a person's ambition, it is unreasonable to expect everyone else to share your same level of vigor. Take time to give yourself, your crew, and actors breathing space. Moreover, unexpected distractions happen often on sets. Factor that into your plan.

As mentioned earlier, you also want to be conscious of company moves. Company moves are the killer to any healthy production. They take a lot of time, and regardless of how fast you can pack, or move in units, they usually take up to several hours to execute efficiently.

I have consulted hundreds of filmmakers who will plan to shoot anywhere between two to five company moves a day, thinking they can get from point A to point F quickly. Ninety percent of the time, the filmmaker falls short and either misses crucial filming material they need, or gets sloppy. Plus the crew and cast get tired and work quality suffers.

On average, it can take a film crew of three to six people an hour to an hour and a half (depending on city) to pack and get from one location to the next. You often see this overreaching schedule on documentary and reality TV shoots, where the producers will have the crew move to four or five locations in one day. Even with limited gear, you are still fighting traffic and other *real-world* conditions that create headaches for the production. In some instances, crew and cast members have gotten into fender benders or forgot gear at locations because they were rushing around. When I see this type of a schedule, I typically run the other direction. It's never worth the stress. This is the main reason I refuse to produce reality TV.

PHASE FOUR

After you have gone through these first three phases, your breakdown can easily be converted into a schedule. The best part of this method is displaying the content in a certain fashion so that if something happens, you can easily flop scenes and (in some cases) even days around to make sure you stay on schedule. Losing a day to bad planning is a disaster.

In this screenshot, you can see the entire production day at a glance. Here we notice that Katie and Brian are on Day 10. On Day 11, Brian is by himself. Seeing it laid out like this helps me make fast decisions when unexpected situations occurs.

For example, if the actress playing Katie calls the day before and says she is sick, I could easily flop Day 10 and Day 11 around. I could shoot all of Brian's solo scenes first to give Katie a day to recover; I could make this decision within a few seconds and quickly notify the actors of the change.

```
------------------    DAY 10 (TUESDAY, MAY 15) (3.50 PAGES) ----------------
124 INT. HOSPITAL RECORDS ARCHIVE - LATER                    59    3 .50
Players: KATIE, BRIAN
Description: Katie and Brian rummage through old medical files. They discover
Amelia was the third daughter.
Props: various banker boxes of old medical files, Brian's I.D. Badge,
indexing labels "A-Z", Hoffman tab, Rolland Hoffman DD2-14, and medical
papers, Whitehall tab, ambulance report from the crash, old black and white
image Walter gave her,
Stunts: N/A
Special Equipment: N/A
------------------ DAY 11 (WEDNESDAY, MAY 16)  (2.50 PAGES) ----------------
96 INT. BRIAN'S APARTMENT / KITCHEN - LATER                  44      .25
Players: BRIAN
Description: Brian arrives home and heads for the refrigerator.
Props: wallet, car keys, beer
Stunts: N/A
Special Equipment: N/A
```

Let me share with you a real story.

A few years ago, I was directing a film where, late in the afternoon, an actress called me and said she was sick. She wasn't really sick, but who was I to argue? Now mind you, she phoned me about two hours before her call time. I had already been on set, filming all day with a handful of other actors at a particular location. Although I had the same actors and location the next day, I decided to move a few things around—so I could accommodate the actress who didn't feel like working that day—while keeping the schedule on track.

I asked my cast, who had scenes with the actress, to flop their shooting-script scenes around to film what they would have filmed the next day instead. I only had about ten minutes to make this decision and was able to do so as a result of my master breakdown and schedule. Had I lingered, mining through all the data that a more sophisticated breakdown would have offered, I would have lost the day and had to pay for more location time, cast, and crew labor.

Knowing your battle plan is key to being a steady hand at the helm of a chaotic indie-production vessel. Your ability to make fast decisions not only makes you a better leader, you will earn respect from your team. Sometimes problems cannot be fixed, but minimizing your problems is more important than the skill of framing the shot, directing the talent, and writing the script. Without your ability to *weather the storm* you will find the filmmaking process a most miserable endeavor.

CHAPTER 5
Locations are Everything

Now that you have successfully crafted a breakdown for your solid screenplay, your next steps should be to find the appropriate locations for your shoot. You want to do this before you start looking for actors. This allows you plenty of time to work out the logistical kinks, and it saves you from settling for places that don't really work for your movie.

I can pretty much guarantee you've heard the term: "Lights, Camera, Action!" The old cliché seems to embody the readiness of the motion-picture process. You can't roll the camera until the lights are ready. You can't shoot a movie without a camera, and your camera doesn't have anything to shoot without actors. However, the term should be modified to say: "Script good? Lights, Camera, Location Ready? Okay, now ACTION!"

Now, it is pretty obvious that you can't make a movie without lights (although these days you actually can), cameras, or actors. But what about locations? Locations are a fundamental aspect of a production checklist. Yet it's the process of production that is most rushed, slopped together, and misunderstood. In fact, most filmmakers that I have met have a rather casual relationship with the task of finding their locations. They put it off until the last minute and often expect the world.

I have a colleague who works for a state-film commission, and she tells me that 90 percent of her location calls go like this:

CALLER: *Hello. I need to find an airport for my movie.*

FILM COMMISSION: *Okay. When is your production?*

CALLER: *On Friday.*

FILM COMMISSION: *This Friday?*

CALLER: *Yes. Oh, and I need it for free. Can you help me?*

I can assume you know what happens next. The caller is usually greeted with a long, dumbfounded silence, a slight chuckle, and sometimes a disconnect.

General lack of location preparation is the single biggest reason most indie movies fail to get off to the right start, or even get made. Location management is the reason I have been able to make six feature films on shoestring budgets and have built a reputation in my community for my professionalism.

It's also important to note that you do not always need buckets of money to secure locations. In some cases, you can find location partners that are more than open to letting you shoot inside their property for a marginal amount of money, or even for free, as long as you can offer some level of professionalism.

But before we begin with the following bullet points, let me make this very clear. You should never expect something for nothing. There is no such thing. The sooner one can remove this ideology from their minds, they will start to be more effective in negotiating fair and realistic terms with people. So let's begin.

Before you start asking around for locations, you should take a self-examination of your situation.

- Can I shoot it in my house, my business, or a family's place?

- Can I afford general production liability insurance?

- Would I be worried about my own production filming at my place if I was the location?

- How much time do I really need in each location?

- How many crew members do I really need at this location?

- Can I pay the location something for their trouble?

FINDING A LOCATION WITH A FILM COMMISSION

One of the most stifling tasks to the location process is where to start. Oftentimes, the location you have in your head is based on some elaborate rendering from your imagination, and it differs vastly from the reality of the world we live in. Finding that perfect location on your own can be difficult, and not knowing the right contacts could keep you searching forever. Luckily, for most cities, states, and municipalities, there are film commissions.

Film commissions are typically state-created agencies that are tasked with helping producers connect with local resources in their jurisdictions. Another function of most state and city film commissions is economic development. They serve as a business perk to incoming productions looking to find local crew, studios, and specialty items, such as catering and insurance brokers. Film commissions can also provide producers with film tax-incentive

113

information and permitting facts. Their main function is to help you locate the things you need to make your film in their community. They want you to film in their state or city and will do everything within their abilities to help you. That said, most film commissions have databases of locations that are film friendly and accessible.

Film commissions, in some cases, can also serve as your advocate and can be instrumental in helping you build outreach in the community you are looking to film in. When I start looking for locations, the first thing I do is research the film commission in the area I am looking to film in. I reach out to their office and ask to meet. I provide the film office with a thorough description of my movie project, as well as budget information and my goals overall. In most cases I'm asked to register my project with their office prior to starting production.

Any time you are asking for help with locations, it's super important to provide as much information on your shoot as possible. This way the film-commission folks can provide you with the right tools that you need for success. If you are not clear on your requests, you may also discover that a location may decide not to help you.

For example, if you have a shoot that requires a gun fight, be sure to let the film commission know this. They will need this information to point you to the appropriate safety measures necessary for permitting and location approval.

If you have production days that require large production trucks to be nearby or on set, this is also vital information.

Oftentimes, filmmakers think that they are being slick by not saying too much about their plans. They later discover, many times while on set, that they are having their access revoked because the location wasn't aware of what they were planning to do. Be as open about what you're doing as possible.

Dear State Film Commission,

My name is Kelly Schwarze and I am with Indie Film Factory in Las Vegas Nevada. My company and I are in the early stages of pre-production on our seventh feature film "It Stares through Dark Shadows". We are seeking office locations for our film and wanted to reach out to you to see about the possibility of helping us secure locations for our shoot.

The film which is PG-13 based in content, is scheduled to film in early August of next year. Our production will take place over the course of three weeks and will require us to film roughly 8-10 hours each day. We have a budget of $200 per day of filming for each location and carry all the appropriate insurances for our shoot. We will also apply for all the required permits and licenses needed to film in your jurisdictions.

Our production is relatively small. We will have approximately 10 crew members and five actors on any given day of filming. We will have one (1 ton) grip truck, a small passenger van, and two picture cars which will be used for some of our exterior scenes. The movie is a supernatural thriller and does not involve any explicit content. However we will have three or four scenes that do require some minor action and weapon props.

If this is you would be willing to assist us with, I can provide you our appropriate insurance documents as well as a copy of the shooting script for review. I am also more than happy to discuss any logistical concerns with you prior to committing to anything.

Thank you for your time and I look forward to hearing from you soon.

Kelly Schwrze
Producer/ Filmmaker
000-000-0000
Email: 0000@000.com

Going the film commission route is my favorite method of finding locations. Not only is the service typically free, but it helps you look more professional when you have the right information for permitting and insurance.

GETTING INSURANCE

For legal reasons, I must be clear that I am not an insurance broker or agent. However, I won't even give the option to not have general-liability insurance for your production. Not having protection is not only unprofessional and dangerous for you personally, but is also negligent toward those who are working for you. The term "Liability Insurance" scares most starting moviemakers. They usually think it's unattainable, or simply not worth the expense. But god forbid if anything happens on your set, you will have more problems than the marginal fee you would have paid for the policy in the first place. The reality is, that production liability insurance is easy to attain, typically affordable, and most necessary.

To start, you should reach out to a licensed broker who specializes in film-production insurance. You can obtain a list of names by searching online or contacting your local film commission. Your policy should cover you for at least for a $1 million. This is the typical minimum for most permitting requirements.

Moreover, if you are working with SAG-AFTRA, you will be also required to have Workers'

Compensation insurance. If you are working with Teamsters, you may also be required to hold *hired auto coverage* for production drivers and equipment associated with transportation—that is, movie cars, production trailers, Star Wagons, and so on.

Depending on the type of movie you are making and the length of the production, your policy can run you anywhere between $1800 and $5000. These policies' premiums may be much more if you're insuring rental equipment, such as cameras, editing computers, media, props, wardrobe, grip trucks, and picture vehicles. Some brokers will offer producers' packages, or bundles, which include your liability insurance, workers' comp, hired auto, rental insurance, and Errors and Omission Insurance (E&O).

E&O insurance is typically a coverage I do not purchase at the time of production. This insurance is dedicated more for the distribution phase of your movie project, and in many cases, your distributor will have this coverage. E&O insurance protects distributors, TV networks, retailers, and the market buyers from any errors made by, or omissions from your movie, whether infringement on someone else's rights, incorrect and false information that is considered libel, or the deliberate or unknown withholding of information regarding your project. I am not a lawyer, so I cannot recommend you not purchasing this coverage. Each project will have its own set of challenges; this is why it's always good to have an entertainment lawyer you can consult throughout the project. We will talk more about lawyers later.

When you contact a broker, they will usually ask you a series of interview questions that help them determine the quote. These types of policies are generally considered "short-term." You may also want to make sure when you are shopping around for insurance, that you ask if you are charged additional fees for "additionally insured" certificates. These are certificates that name the physical location you are filming in. They will be required for most of your locations.

PERMITS ARE A MUST

The term *guerrilla filmmaking* should be a phrase that is stripped from the vocabulary of our textbook. Guerrilla filmmaking is unnecessary and should be frowned upon at every level. In fact, filmmakers can not only be fined for filming without permission, but can be jailed and sued for not having permits. A few years back, a terrible tragedy happened. A young production assistant was working on a film set where she was struck by a train and died instantly. The film crew did not have permission to be on the train tracks where they were setting up, and if not tragic enough, they were told "no" by the company that managed the train tracks. The producers were eventually prosecuted and faced time in prison for their criminal negligence. The moral of this story is to illustrate that there is no reason in the world why this tragedy should have happened. Now, it is not clear why these filmmakers were denied access to their desired location, but one thing is certain: they probably could have found another suitable setting, and with the appropriate permissions could have prevented the loss of life.

In today's turbulent age of mass shootings and terrorism, it's even more of a reason to have permission when filming in public. Gaining access to locations can be surprisingly easier than you think, in most places, and while permit fees vary in cost, you will find the cost of doing things the right way is far less expensive than the other option.

Another great thing about getting the proper filming permissions is that you can film better movies. Filming guerrilla can force you to rush and compromise on quality. Having that permit allows you the control over your creative space and can make your movie look much bigger than it is.

Film permits are typically required for most public lands: streets, spaces, walkways, bridges, military bases, public-service buildings, roads, city and county airports, state buildings, neighborhood parks, schools, state universities, and national parks. Each of these locations may fall in two or more jurisdictions and may require multiple governing bodies to sign off. You may not need a permit if you are filming on private property; however, it's always wise to check with the film commission in your area to see what the rules are. In some cases if the filming set is visible to the public, you may be required to have a permit and police presence, even if you are filming on private property.

When it comes to filming in jurisdictions outside of Las Vegas, I cannot claim to be an expert, but will say that most of the permits that I file are with Clark County, Nevada. This includes the Las Vegas Strip and most of the metropolitan area of Las Vegas. In places like California, permitting can be much more tricky and expensive, depending on what you are looking to do and where you want to film. Some permits will require you to have emergency responders and police presence along with barricades and traffic control. In

Clark County, Nevada, the permitting process is actually very simple. As long as you have the appropriate insurance requirements, you can pull a permit for most filming needs. Although there are certain factors that play into pulling a permit.

A few movies ago, the producers and I wanted a scene shot on the Las Vegas Strip. The scene required the actor to run down a busy lane of traffic after his car overheated. In order to do the scene, I had to have police officers on hand to direct traffic and maintain order. I paid the officers overtime rates, and the fire department also signed off of the permit. The permit required us to shoot the scene early Monday morning around 1:00 a.m. when traffic was slower. The permit cost the production less than $800, and the results were amazing. We pulled off an epic-looking scene on a film budget that was less than most Hollywood catering tabs for a day.

Before you request to pull a permit, my suggestion is to do the following:

Have a detailed description of the scenes you want to film. If it's action sequences, then perhaps have storyboards

If you are looking to block traffic or use public roadways, be sure to include a traffic or route map of your production. This should indicate where your production vehicles will be traveling and where they are looking to slow down, stop, or park.

You should have a head count of crew and an equipment list. Show the permitting officer what you plan to use for equipment and how many people will be on site.

Have the jurisdiction already listed as additionally insured. You can do this even if you haven't filed the permit.

Another point to note in this section is to allow time for the permit. Depending on the complexity of your request, or the number of stakeholders who need to sign off on a permit, it could take several weeks to obtain permission. You may also be required to take safety classes or sign special waivers for the permit, and all of these items do not happen overnight. When I'm looking to film at a public location, I usually start the process several months in advance to make sure everything is in order. I would also advise contacting your local film commission to check all the requirements beforehand. They can also point you in the right direction as to whom you need to speak to apply for the permit.

Starting early on, the permitting process is also a way for you to calculate the cost that will be required to shoot your movie. This information allows you to start pulling together an accurate budget along with your breakdown. It's a safe assumption to say that about 10 percent of your overall budget will go to location fees and insurance. Be prepared and start focusing on setting that money aside.

TAKING CARE OF A LOCATION

For my latest two movies, I shot a majority of the production at a water-treatment facility. In both cases, the movies required underground facilities that were nearly impossible to build or find easily. I reached out to my film commission, and because of the relationship that I had with their office, they made the call for me, asking the water-treatment plant if I could come and scout out the location. With great reservation, the water authorities allowed me to come out and tour their facility. They made it clear to me from the beginning that they would not benefit from allowing film production to be there, and in fact explained why they were apprehensive of allowing to film there. First of all, the facility is a highly sensitive public service, being a water supply for a majority of Las Vegas. Allowing film crews could possibly expose critical infrastructure to the bad guys and present security compromises. Knowing this, I made it very clear that if given permission to film inside their facility, that I would take every possible measure to insure the security and safety of their sensitive location.

After several months of going back and forth with the facility's director, I was given access. I was later introduced to the head of security, who gave my producers and me a tour and outlined all the areas that we were allowed to be in, and all the places that we weren't allowed. My team and I took the initiative to not only adhere to these rules, but to conduct our own briefing for our crew and cast. We made them attend safety meetings with us prior to going onsite. Moreover, we made a point of outlining every detail of what we intended to do while on the property, and we also made a point of including their security chief in every decision we made while on location. After we wrapped we cleaned up our mess and left the place in better shape than we had found it. We also kept the facility and its staff up-to-date on the movie's release, and even invited them to our events and premieres.

Shortly after we filmed our first film there, a big film company came in to shoot some scenes at the facility. The experience was vastly different: they trashed the place, and their crew and cast wandered all over. It was a nightmare for the facility and their staff. After that experience, the plant director decided not to allow any future filming there. So, a few years later when I returned to ask for permission, I faced a new challenge. Luckily, the plant operations manager allowed me to return despite the bad experience they had with the other company. I was later informed that I was the only one they were willing to allow to return. Mind you, I am hounded constantly from other filmmakers to get them in. The location is absolutely the best score in Las Vegas, but because of how I treated the facility, I have earned their trust, and I am now the only one they give permission to.

When filming at a location be sure to do the following:

1. Keep your crew and equipment contained.

2. Clean up after every day of filming.

3. Always ask for permission to move things to alter the setting.

4. **Involve the staff and make them a part of the experience. And feed them.**

5. **Make sure you and your crew are pleasant and friendly, no matter how busy or stressful the days get.**

6. **Leave a positive and lasting impression on the location.**

Keep in mind that in most cases, filming a movie at a location—regardless if it's an indie or a big Hollywood blockbuster—is an exciting experience. It's also important to remember that the people you meet while filming can also become advocates, supporters, and fans of your project when it releases. Build relationships. Never trash a location. You may need it again in the future. Even worse, if you trash it, you mess it up for the next producer.

SOFT MONEY FOR LOCATIONS

The one thing I stressed earlier in this book was that there is NO SUCH THING AS SOMETHING FOR

NOTHING. That being said, I want to dive into the topic of SOFT MONEY. Soft money is a term used to describe items that can be bartered, traded, or lent for exchange, or traded for something other than hard, cold cash. In fact, most indie movies are practically financed this way.

Let me break this down:

You need a classic 1963 Grand Sport Corvette for a shot in your movie. The owner is willing to let you use the car, but not for free. He could probably get anywhere from $300 to $1500 per day for the use of his car. If someone is driving it, it could be even more with insurance. However, you as the indie producer need to save that $300–$500 for sandwiches for the next 10 days of filming. So rather than paying cash for the car, you work out a trade deal. The trade could be to offer the owner of the car a free video, highlighting his prized classic. If you had a day job working for an airline company, maybe you could get him discounted tickets, or offer him your family's or a friend's pass if you had them. Whatever the case may be, you offer the owner something other than money for using his vehicle.

The notion of soft money could also be used for locations, food, props, wardrobe, and in some cases even talent. But before you get too excited, I want to stress that when offering a person or company a trade, you'd better make sure that you can fulfill your end of the bargain, and you offer them something of real value. Many times indie filmmakers will use the term *great exposure* as a bartering chip for soft money. They will tell a potential restaurant location that by participating in their movie and giving up their services or location for free, they will be rewarded with amazing exposure. This trick— and that's really what it is, a trick—is not only unfulfillable, but deceptive. Most people who trade their services or products for this type of deal rarely ever see any exposure or visibility from the movie. That is especially true if the movie is a micro budget. So don't be deceptive. Try to find something that you would want yourself if you were asked. I like to compare this ideology to the holiday game, "White

Elephant," where you bring a gift, and the group picks an unknown gift. And if they like another person's gift better, they can take it from that person and give them their lesser-appealing gift. It's a hilarious game that works best when there are a few lousy gifts in the mix. I was at a holiday party where I bought a really great waffle maker. It was a gift that I hoped I would end up taking home myself. However, by the end of the night, I ended up with a kids' coloring book. The joke was on me! Not that it really mattered, because it was super fun to watch all those gifts trade hands over and over, but I couldn't help thinking, "Man! Someone really made out with my gift!" The moral here is that if you're getting an awesome location, product, or most-needed service for your film, you had better make sure that what you're trading in return is equally cool, if not cooler.

As a videographer and editor, I have given many partners valuable trade for my services, free locations, and catering. In exchange for them working with me, I gave them high-quality commercials and video products that they ultimately used for their own marketing. I traded a service that would have otherwise cost them several hundreds of dollars if they were to hire my company or another.

Soft money is a great option for things that are negotiable, but this method of production finance has its limits. There are some line items that are not negotiable under the soft-money principle. For instance, you would not be able to trade your services for insurance policies, film permits, state licenses, vehicle fuel, copyright registration, or any item that is regulated under law. Moreover, if you are working with a union, they will most likely not be interested in working out a trade deal, especially for cast and crew labor. These items would have to be accounted for and budgeted. You should always consult an entertainment lawyer if you are uncertain about these items.

LOCATION MANAGEMENT

Location management is truly an art. This is why there are specialized people who have the task of not only managing locations, but making sure the set is organized for the production. As an indie moviemaker, your mind is in a million different places; it usually isn't on location management. I had a friend a few years back who was filming a movie that required a junkyard. My friend had secured the location through the owner, Bob. Bob was a great man who was super happy to help my friend with this crucial and pivotal location for the movie. After weeks of phone calls and emails, the day came to shoot the junkyard scene. My friend showed up at 8:00 a.m. along with two gaffers, a handful of PAs, and his camera unit, only to discover the security guard on duty had no idea that they were coming. Bob, unaccustomed to movies filming on his property, had forgotten or simply didn't feel it was necessary to let the security staff know of the shoot.

Despite my friend's best persuasive efforts to explain his case to the guard, there was no movement for several hours. The security staff tried to call Bob, but he had left on a cruise and was not reachable. Not willing to take the producer's word for it, they held their ground and would not permit the production to enter. The day was lost, and it cost the production several thousand dollars, not only for the cost of the day, but to reschedule the shoot. By all accounts it was a total disaster. The junkyard scene was ultimately shot, and it turned out well from what I remember, but it was an expensive lesson for my friend, who had trusted the kind lip service of the owner. "So how is something like this avoidable?" you may ask. It's very simple.

Let me explain.

The number one rule of any location is to make sure you know the personnel on the ground—the security guard, the front-desk clerk, the janitor, the owner's spouse—whomever is going to be the person you meet on the "day of." You should not only have

137

their contact info, but you should have a conversation with them in the days or weeks leading up to the shoot date. Anytime I film on location, I make sure I know all the staff that works the location. I know the security personnel inside and out, and I make sure I have a face to face with them as soon as I get permission from the top. I do this by asking the location management if I can communicate directly with the security staff, to let them know my plans while being on site. This not only shows them that you are professional and honest about your intentions while on property, but protects you from someone not knowing what you're doing. This rule is especially true if you are dealing with small, privately owned locations. This is also very important if you are working with franchises, where there may be several managers and red tape to deal with. When I film on a location, I want everyone in that organization to know I'm coming weeks in advance.

Now this may seem stupidly obvious, but it never fails to surprise me how many moviemakers run into this problem when dealing with locations, and although my friend's story is an extreme example of a communication failure, when these things happen, it slows down the production and can cost you valuable time. Plus, the more you can *get into people's minds* with your project, the less likely they will forget about you. With my last two movies, I had about four physical meetings with the property managers, and over fifty emails and phone calls with the supporting staff leading up to the shoot. It may seem like overkill to some, but I never experienced any communication breakdown on set with the location authorities. Plainly speaking, you cannot afford to leave things to chance. You'd better make sure that the person who is supposed to be unlocking the door and gate is there on time, has the keys, and the right information.

FINDING LOCATIONS THAT NEED LESS SET DRESS

It may go without saying, but the less money and time you have to spend on dressing sets, the more money and time you save for other production headaches down the road. Movie production is about containment of problems, and minimizing those problems will make you an effective and successful moviemaker.

When looking for a location, try to find places that require very little-to-no set dressing. There may be some things you need to place up, like the protagonist's gold metals or pictures of the cast, but if you can avoid having to rent furniture, buy curtains, or set up bookshelves, your wallet will thank you.

CHAPTER 6
Talent is Everything

There's an old notion that the movie is all in the talent. That's really true, especially if you're making a low-to-no budget movie. Finding good actors is an art form that requires a particular skill set called emotional intelligence. I truly feel this is the one area where I excel. When looking at actors to play roles, it is important to understand human behavior and their traits. It's not so much how a person looks or fits a certain mold. It's more about understanding what type of characteristics the actor will emote naturally to the screen. I don't care if we are talking about Robert De Niro, Sean Penn, Helen Mirren, Kate Blanchett or Daniel Day Lewis—they all have particular energies that they display under their act that, no matter what, seep out in a performance. Now this may sound lofty, but there is a language that we all speak that has no words. I'm not talking about body language; I'm talking about energy. We all have energy, regardless if you don't buy into it. We all send off frequencies that can cause people to either like us or hate us, or worse, "meh" us. When casting, it's these qualities that you need to pay attention to the most.

Brian De Palma once said, "The biggest mistake in student films is that they are usually cast so badly, with friends and people the directors know. Actually you can cover a lot of bad direction with good acting."

When searching for talent, it's important to look at the underlining qualities. The most handsome man or gorgeous woman isn't always the best choice. Take for example, Tom Selleck and the *Raiders of the Lost Ark* story. It's well known that he was originally slated for the role of the rugged action-seeker Indiana Jones. However, Selleck couldn't get out of his contract with CBS for the show *Magnum, P.I.* The result was an unassuming Harrison Ford, who happened to be called in to read with other actors. But when George Lucas

142

and Steven Spielberg saw this actor's underlying charm, it was a no-brainer. The idea of Tom Selleck as Indiana Jones is unconscionable, but the lesson of the story is the same. Tom Selleck was the world's sexiest man. He was tall, fit, and had a mustache that would make any man blush. Harrison Ford, by comparison, was plain looking, less fantastic, and a little more of an *everyday* man. The result was a legendary character that every person could relate to. He was clumsy, and real.

When I look to cast for a particular project, I evaluate for the following items:

Is this actor or actress directable?

Does this person know how to perform in front of a camera? (i.e., can they memorize lines, and do they know how to prepare?)

Can this person embody the character I'm looking for? (i.e., if it's an older woman character, can they play that in the physical sense, or can I make them up to look older?)

Is this person easy to work with?

Can this actor be retrained?

Is this actor or actress directable?

The term *directable* in film-industry language means: an actor's ability to be directed in front of a camera. If I ask an actor to do something, can they comprehend it? Can they make adjustments on the fly? Can they take direction to change the outcome of a performance? I have been in many audition sessions where, after enduring a painfully dry monologue, I've asked the candidate to try something different. I'll often ask them to read the monologue again, but this time think about the scene differently. It usually involves me making up a scenario that happened moments before they read the monologue. The goal of this exercise is not only to see if they can do the monologue differently, but if they have the ability to process their emotions along with the text. This helps me understand if this person is able to act based on instinct and emotional faith, rather than trying to perform some cliché of something they've seen on TV or in films throughout their lives.

Here's an example.

If the monologue is about the struggles of adolescence and puberty, then I may ask the candidate to reflect on the idea that they just found out that their first boyfriend—the first person they kissed, the first guy they fell in love with—is now kissing another girl. In the real world, this would be horrific! I am hoping that this trick of the emotions is enough to get the candidate to think differently about the scene they are reading.

Another easy way to see if a person is directable in an audition is to offer them some strong verbs such as "do the scene like you have been running from building to building." The exercise may seem silly and unnatural to the candidate, but it allows you to see how they respond to direction. If they are resistant, then you may have a problem with them if hired.

The bond between the actor and director is one of trust, Both parties have to trust in the other. The actor has to trust in her director, just like the director must trust the actor's instincts in getting them through the scene.

Does this person know how to perform in front of a camera?

On an ultra-low-to-no budget movie, oftentimes, you will be reading (auditioning) actors that have very little or no experience acting in front of a camera. And for the sake of this example, when I say experience, I am not referring to people who have their own YouTube channels or do video blogging. I'm referring to people who have actually read scripted material on camera and have a basic knowledge of camera placement. When casting a very small, locally produced indie movie you typically see candidates that have zero acting experience who have always dreamed of acting, or others who, despite all their efforts, never made it in Hollywood and have spent most of their time in the industry as background extras. You may also notice at this level of filmmaking, the talent pool has more experience with stage acting. Many aspiring actors in local communities have done some form of theater, community plays, or have taken part in some level of acting courses.

Although, let me be clear, I'm not pointing these issues out for the sake of belittling or turning a nose at these types of candidates. Acting is hard, and I have respect for any person, professional or not, who has the courage to try acting and put themselves on the line like that. In fact, in some cases, it's easier to work with these types of candidates than those who think that, just because they shot one scene in a Hollywood movie, they're film stars. I pose the above question more as a way for you (the filmmaker) to understand the candidate's acting discipline knowledge. This can help you make an assessment of how much training you'll need to do with them if they are cast for the project.

Here's an example:

Barbra is great. She looks the part, does well with the script, but she's never actually acted in a movie. Barbra is more of a community-theater actress.

If you cast Barbra for the part, you may need to spend a little extra time training her on the process of filmmaking. Unlike theater, movie acting is a lot of stop and go. Moreover, acting for camera requires actors to be simple. Stage actors tend to overperform due to the nature of emoting for live audiences.

How much time do you have to work with Barbra? Is there someone else who would require less training? Can you even afford to train her?

Now, to be fair to our fictitious Barbra, I've seen people who have had more screen time do worse than those who have never been in a movie. In some cases (not all) the actor who assumes less is easier to shape and mold into the star you're looking for.

What you need to be aware of is how much time a person needs to develop some level of technique for emoting to camera. Acting for camera and stage differs in a variety of ways. One of the biggest takeaways from my own experience is that the actors who have little to no experience on film tend to put the *exclamation point* on a performance. The camera only magnifies that by a thousand. I have a few movies where my actors, despite being marvelous stage performers, came off on screen as overacting cartoon characters. With that experience, I now do what I can to help keep things simple for my actors, so they can forget that they're acting.

When I look at talent resumes, I am searching for candidates who have formal training, some experience on an indie movie, and who look like the person I am searching for. Other than that, it will be up to you as the filmmaker, director, and/or producer to

149

give your preproduction some time to help mold these candidates into functional performers.

Can this person embody the character I'm looking for?

Discrimination is bad. Unfortunately, when making a movie you oftentimes have to look for particular things. Although, I typically like casting opposite of stereotypes, I sometimes have to take into consideration age, gender, race, and body type. However, the main goal for you as a content creator is to find performers who can embody your character. Don't think of what you've seen before, or clichés and stereotypes. Try to look through a filter of personality and spirit.

Let me give you an example of what I'm talking about.

A few years ago I was casting for a movie where I had a nightclub owner. This person was a scary, bad dude. Originally, the producer and I felt the role belonged to a man in his mid to late thirties and of Eastern European descent. However, one day while reading a young woman for another role, I was introduced to something interesting. The woman somehow embodied distrust and disappointment. They were the same qualities that I wanted for the other character. Then it dawned on me that I should try to see how that role looked coming from this woman. I gave the same sides to this lady that I gave to several male actors earlier. She came in and read the same script. Not only did she do a great job with the material, she took the character into a completely different direction. Not only was the experiment interesting, it convinced me to alter that role for a woman. There was something honest and scary about her performance that was absent when the men read it. Although the movie fizzled out at the studio level, I had learned a valuable lesson about focusing on the emotional value of a performer, more so than type.

There's a negative flip side to this. In some cases, you will need the cliché. You need the stereotype. Sometimes the role must be an overweight, grumpy sixty-year-old white man versus a lean and upbeat thirtysomething African American male, and so forth. If you're doing reenactments or historical pieces, you'll obviously need to address the likeness of those you're looking to recreate. It's in these circumstances that you will need to take note and do your best to find people who can service the character if the role requires this.

But allow me to digress from this topic. As an independent filmmaker, it is your duty to find new ways of telling stories and new ways of giving opportunities to others. If you don't then why even do all this? One of the greatest benefits of being your own boss and putting your own money into your business, is that you call the shots. You won't always make the right choices, but the risk and reward of taking chances are much more valuable. No great achievement in this industry has been made by playing it safe. The mavericks of our trade are those who were thought to be foolish in their creative choices, especially when it came to acting.

Hollywood is a marketing industry, not a movie trade. They are in the business of marketing and licensing products. As an indie moviemaker, you have the ability to take risks with your casting, risks that the industry would never dare do. So embrace this advantage and take some risks. The best part of what we're talking about in this book is that the micro-budget movie is nearly impossible to fail as long as you follow a few basic genre and budget moves. Other than that the canvas that you are painting on is yours to create and make a mess of. Have fun!

Is this person easy to work with?

A while ago I was asked about working with difficult actors on set. And I have. In my other profession as a commercial video production company, we have worked with some of the world's most famous faces. Typically the talent is not the challenge; it is the people who surround them. Unfortunately, it's a necessary part of that business. Famous people sell stuff. Famous people are harder to deal with. Bigger corporations are harder to deal with. That's been my experience at least. That being said, on an indie movie, you are the boss. You are the dictator. You get to choose who you work with. You will be married to those people for at least two years, and if they are difficult to be around, your movie experience won't be as much fun.

For me the biggest part of casting is finding folks that you can get along with in order to be creative together. I had a producer friend once advise to me that the biggest part of your job as a producer is to get the actors to trust you and to cooperate. That being said, when looking for actors to fill the ranks of your movie, look for people who are cooperative and positive.

A few years back, I was directing a film where we had hired a so-called veteran actor. The actor had been in a couple of classic movies and was actually pretty talented. Unfortunately his personality left a lot to be desired. He enjoyed telling dirty jokes, which made some of the females on the crew feel uncomfortable,

154

and he berated the other actors, calling them amateurs and wannabes in front of others. He was rude, and his behavior was completely unacceptable. After only two days of filming, he had nearly spoiled the entire spirit of the production and had a few people ready to walk out.

Midway through filming a long and intense office scene, I had enough and ordered the cast and crew to leave the set. I leaned across the desk toward the toxic actor and calmly told him, "I will fire you now. I will call SAG and file a complaint. We will pay you out for the two days you've worked. I will recast this part and shut down this film if I must. I am not afraid to do this. I will not tolerate your behavior any longer."

The stunned man, who was nearly half my age at the time, looked up at me, shell-shocked. I can only assume he had never been called out like that before. He leaned back in his office chair, folded his arms and said under his breath, "What do you need me to do?"

My response was swift, "You fall out of line again, you're out."

We ended up NOT firing the actor, and he never troubled anyone on set from that day forward, or at least not that I was aware of. We ended up finishing the project and everything came out fine. In fact, that film was one of my most cherished experiences. It was the first full feature my wife, Charisma, and I worked on together. We also made lifelong friends on that film that we still work with today. But the moral of this story is that you cannot be afraid to pull the plug; you should not be afraid of pulling someone aside to fix the issue. I was young in my career back then, and I learned a valuable lesson. Knowing what I know now, I would have never cast that actor, regardless of how much experience or talent he had.

We've all heard horror stories of bad behavior from actors. After all, they have a lot of emotional and psychological issues to juggle being an actor. Sometimes crazy personalities are part of the territory.

156

But anytime a person brings down the production or any person on set, it's time to make some changes.

You want to look for actors who are open-minded, people who are good-natured and easy to get along with. You also want honest people and players who take the initiative on their own. There's a sense of entitlement that happens with more seasoned actors, and it can be frustrating on a little movie. However, there are ways you can find positive qualities in your potential cast before you hire them. I typically enjoy doing a couple of table reads, callbacks and actor pair ups before I lock things down. This enables me to see who will not only be punctual, but who is hungry for the part. I want to make sure they are professional and hard working. If a prospective actor gives you lip over having to come back to read with another actor, then more than likely they won't be a team player on set. If they are late to the appointments then I can bet you money that their behavior will not improve when you get on set. I like to think of casting as the first day at spring-training camp in professional American football.

As the coach you're watching to see things that are not so obvious on an initial audition.

Can this actor be retrained?

When working with actors who have little-to-no acting experience, it can be challenging to reprogram years of bad directing from other directors, lofty coaching, and different methodologies. Many actors have attended some form of acting class or have acted in stage performances. In some cases I find it hardest when an actor has done movies with filmmakers who don't understand the creative process of the actor.

Here's an example:

Hank seems to be a good person and a team player. He also seems like he could do the part with a little rehearsal. The only issue is that Hank has done two locally produced short films with student filmmakers. Hank's only experience with direction is when the director of his last two movies would say, "Can you bring that performance down?" or "Can you do that scene again, but this time be a little more angry?" In both instances that is bad direction. Hank has now taught himself that his performance should be measured by intensity, rather than emotion and subtext. By the time Hank gets to your set, he now believes he has all the goods to bring a successful performance. The only problem with that is that Hank doesn't know that he is falling into a trap, the trap of being too actor-ish and campy. If the actor looks like they are acting, then believability of the story dies.

For the sake of this example, I want to point out the bad direction and call to your attention how to redirect your actors into a better mind-set. Most young, first-time directors have never worked with real actors. Therefore, it's a hard lesson to learn when doing a narrative project. The thing about actors is that they want to impress the director. They want to look good on camera. They want to convince the audience of their performance. The real trouble with asking an actor to do something bigger or smaller or angrier is that it doesn't have any subtext or emotional value to it. When you say something like that to an actor, they immediately go into search mode, looking for a mental example of what you're asking them for. It could be an angry father or a sleepy performance from something they saw on TV. Regardless of what they find, it will not be truthful or genuine.

So in lieu of this direction, you should try to use verbs like:

to inspire

to instigate

to seduce

to lure

to steal

to punish

There's a great book on directing simply called, *Directing Actors,* by Judith Weston, and it can give you a much broader scope of directing actors for film. But I wanted to point out this technique in order to outline what you need to look for.

Actors who come from stage also carry some retraining requirements. Stage acting requires you to be *big* and *emote* in a space. Actors can be very theatrical, and when the camera starts rolling they will need to step it back a few paces. In order to retrain your cast, you will need to help them learn to be simple. Less is more. Be careful of overacting or putting *exclamation points* over their head while doing a scene. Keep it simple.

Then there is the actor who has taken two years of acting classes and is now ready for the big time. These candidates can be the most challenging, because they will be resistant to anything that conflicts with the dogma they studied. If they are trained in the *method* way of acting, they can be very difficult to deal with on set. Now to be fair, not all actor training is bad. Obviously it's there for a reason, but an independent film is nothing like the safety of the classroom. The set changes in a flash, and actors are required to think on their feet, and in some cases, improvise.

The main thing in all of these scenarios is that you will need to retrain your inexperienced actor, no matter what. Your job is to mold them into the stars of your film. You will need to teach them how to trust their emotions and learn to adapt quickly. One of the easiest ways to retrain your cast is by doing workshops. Take the time to workshop your actors so you as the director and they as the actor can learn to communicate and trust one another.

If you don't have any previous experience in making a movie, that's okay too. I would suggest workshopping your actors and creating an environment of experimentation. Workshops will be your sandbox, and you will learn to direct them as much as they will learn how to act for your film.

Here is a closing example on working with your actors (although this should be in its own chapter under "the art of direction").

Here is an example of giving actors tools to use their emotions in a workshop:

Jonna is in a scene that requires her to be angry at her husband for maxing out their credit cards at a casino. Jonna comes in, slams the door, and shouts out a majority of her dialogue. Bill, the husband reacts in kind, and a yelling match ensues. Now, on the script, it only says "the couple has an argument." Two yelling actors would be quite the challenge for any audio guy, and it makes for an uninteresting scene over all. You need more dynamics here.

My suggestion would be to pull each actor away so they cannot hear what you're saying to the other. I would tell Bill to think about the idea that he needs permission from Jonna to go on a fishing trip with his long-time buddy, George (although this is all made up). I would pull Jonna aside and tell her to think about the idea that she knows that Bill really wants to go on this fishing trip. I would then put the two actors back together and have them run the same scene.

Although this all hypothetical, and I'm not certain what these actors would actually do, it's highly possible that there would be less yelling. Bill would not want the situation to escalate. After all, he's seeking permission for something he wants. While, Jonna may not need to yell, she knows that Bill wants something, and she's got the control. The scene could be played where both people have an underlying objective, other than getting through the scene and remembering their dialogue.

In doing this you and the actors will discover little ideas and tricks that will make that scene dynamic. Plus, as the director, all you have to do is keep experimenting and making note of what is working. Once you're on set, you can use these things to your advantage. Plus, this exercise is so much fun, because you never know what you're going to get, but it allows the actor to start trusting their emotions and instincts better, and that helps them relax.

CHAPTER 7
Building Your Shot List

Making a movie without a shot list is the same as flying an airplane without navigation or a flight plan. It's crazy! Who knows where you'll end up? The shot list is the most important part of your job as a movie-maker/director. It allows you to visualize your movie shot for shot, and it helps you to work out pacing and editing issues before they happen. Without a shot list, you are going to be fumbling through the process without any discipline or structure. Moreover, shooting without a shot list wastes time and can cause you to miss important shots that are needed to tell the story.

The shot list is a basic outline of the types of shots you will need and the emotional impact it will serve. The shot list doesn't need to be complicated. It can be as simple as writing out a list of scenes for each day of production. But all in all, you must have a plan for what needs to be shot, otherwise your actors and boom operator will be telling you what to shoot. As a director, it's the most important job you have. David Mamet once said, ***"The job of a director is creating the shot list, helping actors be simple and trying not to fall asleep on set."*** This is so true.

Shooting what you need.

Many years ago, I had the distinct honor of hanging out backstage with legendary film director and producer, George Sidney, after he did an interview on my friend's TV show. Mr. Sidney was well into his eighties when we met, but he was still as sharp as a twenty year old. He was known for such classics as *Annie Get Your Gun* (Beth Hutton), *Anchors Away* (Frank Sinatra and Gene Kelly), and *Viva Las Vegas* (Elvis Presley). He had won Oscar awards and was pals with the top names in the history of Hollywood. When I asked what advice he could give to me as an aspiring moviemaker, Mr. Sidney replied, "Only shoot what you need!" At the time I was into my second year

167

of film classes, and everything they taught us was about the economy of filming.

Here's an example:

Film school teaches students to film scenes in the following schedules:

- **Master Shot**

- **Mediums**

- **Medium Close-Ups**

- **Close-Ups**

- **Insert Shots**

Now for most of the process, this makes complete sense. It allows your editor to have plenty of coverage to work with, but what it doesn't factor in is time. Mr. Sidney had started his career in comedy, working on the series, *Our Gang* (a.k.a. *Little Rascals*). He had learned the art of working fast and getting things done simply. And, although he was the patriarch

168

of American musicals, he understood how filming things for the sake of coverage is detrimental to efficiency.

Most coverage that is shot is not used. However, the setups for each of those shots could take hours and, in some cases, even days. When working on a small indie movie, it is crucial that you maximize your camera setups for efficiency and speed. Anytime you have to move a light or a camera, you lose time in the day. For most indies to be successfully shot on a $30,000 to $50,000 budget, you need to film your entire production under twenty days.

What I learned from Mr. Sidney was that if you crafted your shot list like a recipe and took the time to work it out in your head, then you would not only save time on set, but it would allow for faster editing and create money saving wonders.

Another aspect of creating your shot list is for value. If you are limited to the amount of setups you can have in any given scene, then it forces you to intellectualize what the shot is about and what it is saying. Every shot in the movie should say something other than simply capturing dialogue or action. Shots should be in juxtaposition of one another and should propel the story forward through visuals.

Below is a sample of a scene that takes place around a kitchen table. I'd like to start by saying table conversations are among the hardest scenes to shoot. But if you look at this sample, you will see how I aimed to create tension between the characters while pushing the expository of their pasts into the sideline of the scene. In fact, this scene isn't really about them catching up; it is about deception and concealing the truth.

A little backstory on this scene: In an earlier scene, Brian eavesdropped on Katie's conversation with her ex-boyfriend. He thought she was done with that guy but he is now wondering if she really is.

Take a look:

```
76      INT. DINING ROOM - NIGHT                            76
        Red wine pours into a plastic red cup. Moving back, Brian
        empties a screw top bottle of its last drop --

                            BRIAN
                    -- tried calling you earlier. I
                    didn't know if you liked red or
                    white... or whiskey.

        Katie hovers over the cramped electrical stove stirring in
        what looks like meatballs and red sauce.

                            KATIE
                    Yeah its okay... had to get a new
                    phone. The other one crapped-out on
                    me.

        Brian references the comment with a suspicions glare. He
        takes his seat and hits a nervous sip from the plastic cup.

        Katie arrives with the food -- a steaming pot of sauce, and a
        strainer filled with spaghetti noodles. She drops to her seat
        --

                            KATIE (CONT'D)
                    Hope this doesn't kill you. I don't
                    really cook a lot.

        Brian wastes no time digging in. He plops a plate full of
        noodles and goes for two servings of red sauce --

                            BRIAN
                    How bad can you mess up spaghetti?

                            KATIE
                    Let's find out...

        Katie tosses the oven mitts to the other side of the table.

                                                    CUT TO:
```

Convention would tell us to shoot a wide shot of the entire scene, then move to Kate's mediums and close ups, and eventually getting Brian's lines. That would be a total of seven set ups, plus the inserts. However, at that rate we would be drawing attention away from what the scene is really about. It's about them hiding something. No one really cares about the small talk. The only thing the audience should care about is if they are going to call each other out for lying. By keeping my audience off balance, it allows me to keep them hooked. See what I did here:

76   INT. DINING ROOM - NIGHT   76

Red wine pours into a plastic red cup.

[STATIC SHOT - INSERT SHOT - EXTREME CLOSE UP]

Moving back, Brian empties a screw top bottle of its last
drop --

                         BRIAN
                -- tried calling you earlier. I
                didn't know if you liked red or
                white... or whiskey.

Katie hovers over the cramped electrical stove stirring in
what looks like meatballs and red sauce.

[STATIC SHOT - KATIE PROFILE IN FOREGROUND FILLING ENTIRE
LEFT SIDE OF FRAME, BRIAN STANDING IN THE BACKGROUND CENTER
FRAME - BRIAN IN FOCUS]

                         KATIE
                Yeah its okay... had to get a new
                phone. The other one crapped-out on
                me.

[SAME SHOT AS PREVIOUS - PULL FOCUS TO KATIE AS SHE SPEAKS]

Brian references the comment with a suspicions glare.

[REVERSE ANGLE - BRIAN NOW IN THE CLOSE UP REACTING TO
COMMENT, WHILE KATIE IS IN THE BACKGROUND COOKING AT THE
STOVE. BRIAN LOOKS DOWN TO THE TABLE. KATIE GLANCES OVER
NOTICING HIM LOOK DOWN]

He takes his seat and hits a nervous sip from the plastic
cup.

Katie arrives with the food -- a steaming pot of sauce, and a
strainer filled with spaghetti noodles. She drops to her seat
--

                         KATIE (CONT'D)
                Hope this doesn't kill you. I don't
                really cook a lot.

Brian wastes no time digging in. He plops a plate full of
noodles and goes for two servings of red sauce --

                         BRIAN
                How bad can you mess up spaghetti?

                         KATIE
                Let's find out...

2.

```
Katie tosses the oven mitts to the other side of the table.
[WIDE STATIC SHOT, FRAMING THE COUPLE BEWEEN THE WALLS THAT
LEAD TO THE KITCHEN ENTRANCE]
                                        CUT TO:
```

If you notice, this simple and slight arrangement of shots forces the audience's attention away from the mumbo jumbo of the dialogue and, instead, to the subtext of the scene, which is about Brian trying to see if Katie will be honest about what she's hiding, or if she will continue to deceive him. Here is an explanation on why I choose those shots:

76   INT. DINING ROOM - NIGHT   76

Red wine pours into a plastic red cup.

[STATIC SHOT - INSERT SHOT - EXTREME CLOSE UP]

*(I did this to establish the character's need for calming his
nerves. He knows Katie is hiding something, and most likely
thinks alcohol will help with his investigation)*

Moving back, Brian empties a screw top bottle of its last
drop --

                   BRIAN
           -- tried calling you earlier. I
           didn't know if you liked red or
           white... or whiskey.

Katie hovers over the cramped electrical stove stirring in
what looks like meatballs and red sauce.

[STATIC SHOT - KATIE PROFILE IN FOREGROUND FILLING ENTIRE
LEFT SIDE OF FRAME, BRIAN STANDING IN THE BACKGROUND CENTER
FRAME - BRIAN IN FOCUS]

                   KATIE
           Yeah its okay... had to get a new
           phone. The other one crapped-out on
           me.

[SAME SHOT AS PREVIOUS - PULL FOCUS TO KATIE AS SHE SPEAKS]

*(Both of these previous lines are in one shot. The frame is
to make her look larger than him. She's the one hiding
something, and holds all the cards. He is smaller in the
frame being in the background. He is the one trying to
achieve something. All Katie has to do is play stupid)*

Brian references the comment with a suspicions glare.

[REVERSE ANGLE - BRIAN NOW IN THE CLOSE UP REACTING TO
COMMENT, WHILE KATIE IS IN THE BACKGROUND COOKING AT THE
STOVE. BRIAN LOOKS DOWN TO THE TABLE. KATIE GLANCES OVER
NOTICING HIM LOOK DOWN]

*(In this situation, the audience knows Katie is covering
something up, and they know that Brian knows this too. What's
interesting about this set up is that once Katie reacts to
Brian looking down to the table, after hearing her lie about
her phone, the audience is now introduced to a new conflict.
Katie knows that Brian is suspicious about something)*

He takes his seat and hits a nervous sip from the plastic
cup.

The shot list is easy to follow. I could give it to
any person on set, and they could understand what
needs to be done.

However, if I shot the scene in the traditional sense, it could take upward of six hours, leaving the editor with a monotony of angles and footage to sift through, which would slow down the editing process. Using the "only shoot what you need" method, I was able to shoot this scene in under an hour. Plus my scene was much more interesting, and the efficiency allowed me to shoot more scenes in a day.

The shot-list process should also be enjoyable. In some cases you may not know what to do with it or where to start. I always suggest to first-time filmmakers: steal from the greats. Look at other works of art and take notice of the editing. Two scenes that come to mind are the foot chase in the original *Point Break,* directed by Kathryn Bigelow, and the *MILLENNIUM FALCON* aerial-combat in *Star Wars IV: A New Hope,* directed by George Lucas. In *Star Wars IV: A New Hope*, Lucas cut together World War II documentary footage of many dogfight sequences, which he ultimately used in creating the iconic climax in his masterpiece. In *Point Break*, Bigelow stripped down her

176

production to create exciting movement and speed. Not only did they have to figure out how to rig cameras for this sequence, but they also had to outline every shot and cut beforehand. The end results are astounding, and most people will never know that several weeks, and possibly months, went into planning these historical moments in cinema. But, since they did all the hard work, no sense in trying to reinvent the wheel on your first go. Study these scenes forward and backward, and see if there are any elements you could use for your shot list.

In the end, don't make your movie until you work it out on paper. It will save you time, money, and stress. The best part of this process is that a shot list can adapt to any location. So don't use the excuse that you can't make a shot list because you haven't seen the location. The location, while very important, is inconsequential for this process. The goal is to get you to think in terms of visual storytelling. The more you are forced to agonize over every shot, the better your film will be for the audience. But if you do this exercise (which could take months), you will fly through your production once you're on set. Best of all you will be decisive and know exactly what you want. Crew and actors love that, by the way!

CHAPTER 8
Making Your Movie with Less

I remember strolling through the American Film Market for the first time nearly twenty years ago. I took notice of the all the questions regarding budget. At that time I was shopping a little action film I wrote, directed, and produced, called *The S.I.N.* Now, let me be real about this; the movie was by far my worst work. The acting was horrible, the shots were bad, and the story was better suited for a TV show. The one thing we had going for us was the sound. We had great sound equipment loaned to us by a colleague. Sound was crucial to getting a decent movie sold—or so I thought. I shuffled the crowded hallways of the Lowes Hotel, in Santa Monica, California, mesmerized by all of the movie art and the people. But every time I stopped to introduce myself and my movie, I was hit with the same three questions from distributors:

What was your budget?

Who's in the movie?

What did you shoot it on?

At the time I was pitching a movie that cost $5000 to make, had no name actors in it, and was shot on a mini digital-video camera I bought from my local electronics' shop. It was a recipe for immediate rejection, and that was pretty much what I received. That experience had taught me that the industry cared very little about the story or your best efforts. All they cared about was those three things. **BIGGER = BETTER.** One distribution-representative laughed at me when I told him that my movie only cost $5000. I had another lady tell me to go back to the drawing board with it. One distribution company actually asked my partner and me to leave their office to make room for more important filmmakers. The experience not only frustrated me but inspired me to pave a new path forward for my movies.

As I stood holding a bag of screeners in my hands, I looked around at all the self-absorbed people, pushing, clamoring, and fighting to make a deal. It absolutely disgusted me. What was even worse was how filmmakers prided themselves on how much money they had for their budget. I had met two filmmakers that day who had claimed their movies cost over $1 million to make. They were most likely lying about it, but the moral of this story is the same. Bigger, at least **bigger sounding = BETTER.**

So I thought about it long and hard on the way back to my home in Las Vegas.

"What if I could make something that looked like a million bucks? Would that matter? And if so what if I could do it for a fraction of most movies?"

The wheels were spinning. It was at that moment that I grew from being a wannabe movie maker into an entrepreneur. I couldn't help but laugh, thinking that some of the screenings and previews I had seen from creators claiming their films cost so much actually looked worse than the movie I had shot for only $5000!

Could it be that I knew how to fake it better, or was there something I had that no other moviemakers had?

Whatever it was I was determined to create a company that specialized in micro-budget movie making. I figured, if we could make movies quickly and in the least expensive way, surely we could find a market for them and make money in the meantime. I mean, after all, isn't that how old Hollywood started anyway?

Another thing I knew for certain was that I did NOT want to owe an investor money. I had met so many producers that week at the American Film Market, who were on the hook for hundreds of thousands of dollars, and most of them were in exactly the same situation I was in. They didn't have a distributor. Most of the people I had met had borrowed money from family or friends who more than likely would never see their money back. Some of the movies I saw being pitched had a few name actors in them, but even so, I wondered if they would actually find success. Another interesting side note I learned from that experience was that getting a distributor to pick up your movie in no way guaranteed you'd ever make a dime back on your film.

It's almost laughable now to think that movies were rejected because they cost too little to make. I mean, who cares? The interesting fact in today's market is that it doesn't matter if you have a movie that cost $10,000 or $1,000,000. You are still going after the same buyers. With VOD and an oversaturated market, movies are clamoring for visibility. In fact, my movies are on the same shelves as studio movies. My last title, *Alien Domicile*, was the only non-studio title released on Redbox in the month it was released, and it was available among all the other movies that cost a thousand times what I spent making it.

Even more puzzling, the micro-budget movies are getting the same deals as the medium-tier budgets on places like Amazon, Hulu and Netflix. And unless you are a huge studio picture or have some major film-festival prestige, you are just another movie in the bargain basket. According to several distributors that I've spoken with, a non-studio indie movie is lucky to see a return of $200,000 within their first five years in the market. That's basically earning $40,000 in sales each year. Think about that! You have a product that is only making $40,000 a year and you more than likely need to share a majority of that with the people selling your product. So even if you are doing a *gross deal* with a distributor at a 50–50 split, you would only be bringing home $20,000 in the year. This is crazy! So by my calculations, if you had a movie costing $150,000, it would take you a little over seven years to make your money back, and that's if your sales company continues to push your product year after year.

Now I'm not a genius, but I'd say that situation sucks. Wouldn't you like to keep most of that return the first year instead of having to shell out every dime you see for seven plus years back to investors? I think so. That's why I love micro-budget filmmaking. In my humble opinion, I consider micro-budget filmmaking to be the future of cinema. I see micro-budget filmmaking as the only alternative to true independent producers. So what is a micro-budget film? Well that number has gone up quite a bit over the last two decades, but I consider micro budgets those ranging between $10,000 and $50,000. The return on investment (ROI) is usually much faster, and seven positive things happen when you make movies on this low of a budget.

1. You usually make your money back.

2. You typically make money on the investment.

3. You can continue to make more movies.

4. You don't have to hide from angry investors, or grandmas.

5. You can typically self-finance your movies, maintaining power and control over your work.

6. You can build a volume of content, which some day could be valuable as a body of work.

You're nearly immune to bad market years and failure.

A few cool kids that I've crossed paths with—who were shooting movies for $100,000 or more—have sputtered out after they failed to breakeven in the marketplace. And to be fair, there are such things as *bad deals*, which we will cover in the following chapter. But that aside, the marketplace is really changing fast. In fact it has probably changed since you started reading this book. This being an oversaturated market has also driven down the price most buyers are interested in paying. The truly tragic part of this story is that many producers who, after successfully securing the funds to make their $100k–$500k movie, securing named talent, and crafting a solid film, will be seen as failures—not even taking into account that the current

186

distribution market is collapsing. Most of these talented filmmakers end up never shooting movies again—or they have to come down to my playing field.

All market signs seem to point to a new world of content creating and distribution, where filmmakers will have to rely primarily on the *in-content* advertising model to see any income for their movies. It will be similar to music platforms like Pandora and Spotify. Revenue returns will shrink, and content creators will have to be more clever in creating themselves as a brand. The movies they create will only be a part of their overall business plan.

If you don't believe me on the above, just ask any content creator who was a part of Amazon Video Direct (AVD) platform prior to March 1, 2018. Prior to what I like to call *BLACK MARCH*, creators were earning fifteen cents per minute streamed domestically and six cents internationally on AVD. It was a fair rate and allowed content creators to see a little cash flow each month for their efforts. But as of March 1, 2018, the retail giant decided they had enough of paying this royalty rate, so they reduced royalty earnings by nearly 50 percent by creating a tier system that starts every title out at six cents per minute streamed. And yes, these included the big guys. Creators went from making anywhere from fifty to twenty dollars a month on any given title to making less than five dollars a month.

The new rules require filmmakers to reach over a 100,000 hours streamed within a year in order for their royalty rates to be paid at ten cents per minute streamed. That's nearly impossible for most average filmmakers to reach unless they have major marketing budgets, or simply get lucky. And even if they did reach 100,000 hours streamed in a year, they'd have to get to 500,000 hours streamed in that same time frame to get back to the rate they were getting paid previously. I would suspect that most independent filmmakers will now be looking at six cents per hour streamed indefinitely, which is a dramatic decrease in revenue.

You would make more money selling recycled bottle caps.

The moral of all this is KEEP YOUR BUDGETS LOW. I couldn't imagine if I had movies that were dependent on AVD bringing home the bacon. I know some moviemakers out there are hurting big time. If you want to make anything higher than a micro-budget movie, you're playing Russian roulette. The only way I would even consider doing a pricier picture is if I were hired on to do so or was working on a studio or industry-financed project. They have the money to push the product. Everyone else, no matter who you have signed on for talent, will have to use social media and hope they get a response from audiences. It's a crapshoot that leaves you too much liability and not enough control over your own destiny.

HOW TO KEEP YOUR BUDGETS LOW

So let's talk about how to keep your budgets low. Here are a few tips to recap:

Economy of scale: Make a movie that requires limited locations, talent, and expensive scenes, props, etc.

Soft Money: Use soft money, such as services trade to get props, wardrobe, catering, and in some cases, locations.

Take a back-end: Don't pay yourself right now. Pay your talent and crew first. Pay the people that you need to help you get the movie done. If you make a movie for $50,000 then you should be able to recoup within a year or so and put some money back into your pocket.

Nonunion: Find good actors and stay away from unions for now. Although I am not antiunion, I am prosavings. Unions, despite their best efforts to help moviemakers, are not designed to have your best interest in mind. SAG-AFTRA is a fantastic union for talent if you have the money to pay. And no matter what type of low-budget agreement you sign, it will be a nightmare for your little micro movie. Save unions for your dream project.

Less is more: Don't get caught up in having lots of people and crew on set. Only hire who you really need. That's a *cameraman, audio person, script supervisor, one or two grips,* and a *handful of PAs.* Keep your team and equipment light so you can move fast without tripping over each other.

Preproduction is everything: Make your movie on paper first. Plan. Plan. PLAN! Know your shots and have them ready to execute.

Saving conscious: Look for savings in every way; food, props, locations, set dressing, equipment rentals, and simplicity of filming.

Limited shooting days: Only shoot 15-20 days.

DIY editing: Do your own editing. If you don't know how to edit, now is the time to learn.

Multiple hats: Get good at wearing multiple hats. You may be able to save your production thousands of dollars by working on things yourself.

Don't be afraid to start: Most young filmmakers wait for conditions to be perfect for them. Don't be afraid to make mistakes and learn from them. Just get going!

Working with the idea to keep things low cost is the best way to start positioning yourself into an actual business. Your goal should always be to make your movie as close to zero as possible, obviously never skipping on filming requirements, permits, safety, food, and crew/cast satisfaction. Lastly, aim to make a movie that you know you can make. Focus on your talent as a moviemaker. You can only get better if you are doing it often, so create that *often* filmmaking experience in your life!

CHAPTER 9

Finding Distribution: LET THERE BE NO MORE SECRETS

Each year hundreds of people enroll in film-studies' programs across the United States. Little do they know that their efforts of becoming great filmmakers rely very little on the amount of technical and philosophical schooling they receive in these programs. Many film programs base their curriculum on technique, application, and theory, and as important as these areas of studies are, they fail to address a bigger issue with our industry.

How do I make money doing this?

In fact most film studies do a better job at teaching students how to get technical or administrative jobs in the industry, but fail to educate minds on how to actually become entrepreneurs. I dropped out of college because of this. And although I now teach at a collage,

193

I dedicate my syllabus to forcing this point. Filmmaking is a business. Going to Hollywood and getting a job in the industry is another.

The goal of this entire book is to help people be filmmaking entrepreneurs and create the things they want to create and then profit by it. Without a proper understanding of the business, and without a clear goal of what you desire to achieve, you may find yourself burning out on this career path within a few years. Sadly this is what happens to a majority of film students who fail to land jobs in this forever-turbulent entertainment landscape.

Filmmaking, from its conception, was designed as an artistic medium for commercial enterprise. From the first moment the Lumière Brothers frightened a crowd of Parisians with the images of a train, to Thomas A. Edison patenting the movie camera in New York as his own, filmmaking has been and always will be a marriage of commerce and spectacle. We often confuse filmmaking with the term *Art*. Art in general is

194

subjective by design. Although movies can also be subjective (meaning liked by discriminatory taste), the movie business has found a way to balance its alter ego with solid market practices.

There is a huge myth out there that Hollywood has flops. Hollywood does not have flops. They have weak openings, false starts and slow learners, potential losers, but never flops. Take even the lowest-grossing box-office films of the last twenty years, and you will see that even the so-called losers are profit makers in the long term. Not only do they ultimately recoup their budgets, but they go on to profit well into movie geriatrics.

Take for example, *John Carter*, directed by Andrew Stanton in 2012 (and despite some arguments over this number) Disney allegedly spent $250 million on this film, and it was considered dead at arrival. It was called a flop by the critics and the industry gurus before it had even had a full two days at the box office. Despite this the film has gone on to gross $280 million worldwide and counting. Plus it taught the Mouse House a valuable lesson on developing lesser-known content, which has seemed to service them well ever since. Box office and opening earnings are only headline grabbers. Don't pay attention to this.

So why am I bringing it up? I did this to point out that the movie business—despite its luster and glitz—is a product that with a little marketing savvy, smart development strategies, and persistence can be an underdog success story. Think of movies like real estate. I have a movie that flopped when it hit the market back in 2015. It could not find an audience to save its life. No one cared, and nobody really supported the film. Nearly five years in the market, this movie is slowly gaining traction and making sales. In fact it leads the sales reports over newer titles in my library. Sometimes films do not strike when they are released. Sometimes they filter to the top after a long journey. So, do not fret.

No matter what type of creative career path you are in, you must answer the following questions:

Who is my audience?

What do they like?

How can I make something they can use and enjoy?

These questions pertain to the music business, literature, sculpting, dance, poetry, and filmmaking. We have all heard the expression, "*I don't do it for the money. I do it for the art.*" I hate this expression. It's foul, lazy, and uninspiring. The notion that financial achievement and art cannot coexist is a lazy person's excuse. They lack understanding of the human experience altogether. Nothing of great achievement can be accomplished without the rewards of finances, body, mind, spirit, and health. Those who live in poverty while trying to create are not living in the rewards of finances, body, mind, spirit, and health. Some argue that a starving artist's struggles can be valuable fuel for creativity. But I suggest that it cannot sustain enlightenment and desire over the long term. Think of some of the most famous painters of all time. Despite their masterpieces very few of them lived a healthy and rewarding life. Many of them never got to see the value of their art while living, and most of them had one tragedy and heartbreak after the other. There are some who believe their art is bigger than their life itself, and I can appreciate that, but it's certainly not for me. I love life, and I desire to see the rewards of my creative endeavors while I can enjoy them.

You must be able to thrive in life with your passion and your talent, regardless if your aim is to become the next rich and famous film director or simply to provide the basics of life for yourself and family. The level of finances is inconsequential, but you have to earn money doing your thing, otherwise it's just a hobby. Hobbies are great for passing the day, but they will never resonate to anything meaningful for the world at large if they cannot be more than a time killer.

The reason the term *starving artist* permeates in today's world, and the reason most people do not consider filmmaking a serious career choice, lies in the lack of business consciousness and marketing savvy. In fact, when it comes to filmmaking, marketing and business mindfulness is nearly 80 percent of the experience in making a motion picture. The creative faculties are second priority in the development of a movie project. Now this is by no means to diminish the importance of creativity, uniqueness, and/or quality. But it is a fact that without marketing and business strategy, a film project—no matter how unique, clever, and well-produced it is—will fail.

Hollywood, for better or for worse, has managed to make this example a science, and has made movies and movie making one of the major players in gross domestic products. The motion-picture industry generates more money than some small countries: more than the finance and banking industry and more than telecommunications and real estate. Yet a career path in the motion-picture arts could get your parents to disown you.

The reason most budding filmmakers fail isn't their misunderstanding of cameras, camera angles, screenwriting, editing, or knowing what looks good. It's not understanding the market they are trying to break into. Nearly every indie filmmaker I have met is so foreign to the word *distribution* that it makes them sweat when the subject comes up. Most students have given little to no thought on the matter, and their instructors couldn't tell them the first thing about the subject.

Why? Why isn't the film market taught as Filmmaking 101? Why are distribution courses not required before getting a film major?

Now this may sound like a conspiracy theory, but it is my belief that Hollywood has clouded the facts of how it makes money so well that it keeps many economists and business scholars puzzled. They all understand how the traditional Hollywood model works, but most professionals remain puzzled on how independent companies, smaller studios, and independent producers can profit in today's changing landscape. The marketplace is not only unpredictable and fickle—shrinking then expanding—it's also ever-evolving, and the rules change nearly every week. The once liberators of independent film are now the oppressors, and the cycle starts all over again. Moreover, it's the least-regulated industry in the United States, yet it makes more GDP than the banking industry. Go figure. Distribution companies have no code of ethics to follow, and many moviemakers have fallen prey to bad deals and predatory practices that the industry at large turns a blind eye on.

However, this chapter—which is the last chapter of this book—is the most important text I have ever written. I have spent my entire adult life trying to find a way forward with distribution, not only of my works, but to help other content creators free themselves from the shackles of market ignorance. Although things are changing constantly, there are a few basics that could turn the most average producer into a profitable businessperson. Like many of you reading this book, I knew very little about distribution when I first started, and there was nothing out there to help me. I was conned by a few companies early on and had to learn the hard way. But before I learned from the *school of hard knocks*, I had the same thinking that many of you may have had.

"If I can make a movie and get it into a film festival, then everyone will love me. I'll be rich and famous! Just gotta make my masterpiece!"

That seems to be the business plan for many young content creators and, surprisingly, even those who have made a few movies. The only thing I can guarantee with this strategy is absolute heartache. But after you read this chapter, I promise you that a whole new mindset will appear to you and, for better or worse, you will look at the industry differently.

Please take careful note of this chapter and read it more than once. Keep it bookmarked so you can access it easily later. And if the time comes for you to use it in practice, take the time to read it again before contacting your entertainment lawyer. Take into account that every piece of information I am presenting to you has been tested and applied in my own business. And no matter what others may try to tell you about film distribution, I can promise that the items I am covering in this chapter will service you the best with this topic. It will keep you safe, help you earn some money from your endeavors, and allow you to be wiser than the sharks that prey upon indie filmmakers.

Let me also stress that it is not my intention to create a negative picture of the indie- and micro-budget film-distribution industry. This business has its heroes and villains like any other industry. It is my goal to help you seek out good distribution partners and find common ground as a entrepreneur. It is my task to help you create meaningful and mutually beneficial relationships with the people who are selling your film. The actual truth is that you need distribution partners as much as they need you. Without each other there would be no commerce or growth.

In this chapter I will be covering the following topics:

- *What is a film market?*
- *What distributors look for.*
- *How film distribution works.*
- *Never be afraid to walk away from a bad deal.*
- *Finding the right lawyer.*
- *The contract: good deals vs. bad deals and what to make sure is in them for yourself.*
- *How to find a distributor.*
- *Deliverables.*
- *The future of distribution and alternatives.*
- *Marketing and audience building.*

What is a film Market?

By definition film markets are trade events where business is conducted for the purpose of finding distributors, financing partners, and selling films to different territories. There are over a dozen serious film markets that take place across the world each year. These markets include Cannes Film Market, Berlin, Asian Film Market (the other AFM), MIPTV, and American Film Market (AFM). Some film festivals have also become film markets within their own right, such as Sundance, SXSW and Toronto. The purpose of these markets is to bring buyers and sellers under one roof to make deals and map out the landscape for the next season of commercial-entertainment content.

Without boring you with the details of each of these markets, I will say that most of these events are more or less trade shows or industry conventions. I'm sure we've all been to one or another, but trade shows like Consumer Electronics Show (CES), Comic-con, in San Diego, are similar examples. There is nothing sexy or too exciting about these events. I point this out to take away the prestigiousness of the term *film market*.

WHAT FILM SCHOOLS DON'T TELL YOU / SCHWARZE

Many moviemakers are mystified by this term, and just the subject is intimidating.

These markets are packed with various company booths where products and swag are displayed like a toy store. Walls are wrapped in bigger-than-life movie posters, and actors walk the floors dressed up in famous character costumes. Typically the same buyers and sellers are at each event, with a few regional exceptions, and production companies sometimes host elaborate parties to drive up the hype for their products. Anyone can attend these events for a price. The average fee for the American Film Market, in Santa Monica, California, runs from $300 to $1500, depending on what badge you purchase. The higher-tier badges can offer you unprecedented access to the industry's top movers and shakers, as well as fantastic lectures, parties, and networking events.

That all said, it's important to note that having a strategy before attending one of these markets is key.

Most of the time, you must have a meeting scheduled to physically meet with buyers or distribution companies, at least the good ones. It's crucial to have scheduled meetings in advance and to have your completed film, trailer, synopsis, and any other visual collateral ready to go in order to pitch your work. In some cases producers will employ sales agents to negotiate on their behalf. These individuals should understand the market and know the best possible route to success for your project level. I would suggest the following before making plans to attend a film market:

Step one: Do some research on the companies that are attending the market. Also, find companies that are in-line with the type/genre of film you are making or have made. So for example, don't waste time with Company X that only distributes Christian films when you have a *slasher* flick. It won't work.

Step two: Send prospective companies an email along with a link to your trailer (hopefully you have one) and request a meeting during the event. If they are interested, then they will schedule something.

If you do not line up a meeting, then you should re-evaluate your strategy and goals for attending. These events can be very expensive, and if you cannot maximize your productivity at one of these markets, maybe you shouldn't attend. Moreover, you can always connect with distribution companies after the market closes. You don't necessarily need to attend a film market in order to secure distribution for your movie. It's just a good excuse to have a face-to-face. That said, it has been my experience that many of the companies that are hard to lock down at these markets tend to loosen up and be more reachable after the market closes. This is because many of the reps that work for these companies are slammed with stuff leading up to the market. Reaching out to a distribution company a couple weeks after a market closes is my best advice if you cannot attend the market itself.

Attending a film market should also be approached with caution. I never advise producers to sign deals on site, and you should always contact the appropriate legal consultation before entering any agreement. Moreover, you should also have a clear understanding of your goals, whether to find exposure for yourself as a filmmaker, raise money for a project, find talent, or to make your investor's money back.

What distributors look for

You know, there is a lot of nonsense out there about what companies are looking for. There are some gurus who proclaim that you can't sell your movies without star power, nudity, sex, violence, action, talking dogs, or without having some big social media presence. It's all nonsense. Now, there are some companies that will not look at titles with no stars attached. This is true. Moreover, as discussed in chapter 2, genres do play a part in finding success in the market, and some companies may look for more aggressive titles. But let me offer a few points that are total deal breakers for many established micro-budget distributors:

A. **Movies with bad sound.**

B. **Movies with too much explicit content, such as violence, sex, drugs, and/or are close to NC-17 in nature. They can't sell to most retailers.**

C. **Movies that carry offensive political, racial, or ideological values.**

D. **Movies that are slapstick comedy (unless you do have stars).**

E. **Movies that have bad lighting, total amateur acting, bad camera work, and shoddy production value overall.**

The goal for you as the content creator is to avoid all of these pitfalls during the writing and development process. If you design a project that stays clear of these "Do-Not's," you will have a better chance at locating distribution for your film after the fact. It just makes things easier.

How distribution works

Most creatives I work with have completed micro-budget films and are looking for distribution after the fact. I like to call this *postdistribution,* meaning they made the film without a distribution agreement in place and are shopping the completed film in hopes to land a deal. Finding distribution for a completed movie should be pretty straight-forward. At least you would think, ***"Find a distributor and the rest is history, right?"*** Wrong! Unfortunately this is where most filmmakers fail miserably. Some of them end up never making another movie after this experience. They fail to understand that finding a distributor is just the beginning, and in some cases, the greatest challenge of it all. Making the film is the easy part.

Allow me to offer a comparison of what people think the process of distribution is like, versus what it ends up being for many microfilmmakers .

This is most people's understanding of micro-budget film distribution:

Step One: The moviemaker brings their movie to a distributor.

Step Two: Distributor sells the film to its buyers, attends the markets, and makes the deals. Meanwhile, the moviemaker lies on a beach somewhere.

Step Three: Distributor pays the moviemaker a share of the profits. Everyone is happy. Moviemaker is famous...oh, and rich!

But of course, this is not the reality.

Micro-budget film distribution actually goes like this for many micro-budget filmmakers :

Step One: The moviemaker brings their movie to a distributor. They sign a boilerplate deal, sometimes with the misguidance of an entertainment attorney. The distribution company request a bunch of deliverables, which the moviemaker stresses out over, because they didn't know they needed all this stuff. This takes several weeks to finalize, and the moviemaker has to go back and re-edit his movie to make the deliverables list. *(We will talk more about this later.)*

Step Two: Distributor takes all the rights to the film, even rights it won't use.

Step Three: The distributor takes the film to market and bundles the moviemaker's movie with another dozen or so titles. They sell the bundles to their buyers and collect a flat fee for each of those deals, which is ultimately absorbed by the distributor's so-called expenses. If there is any money left over after the distributor takes out their expenses (and there is rarely anything left), then they will split whatever is left between the other films in that bundle. All of this is happening while the moviemaker is on the beach.

Step Four: The distributor sends out reports each quarter and deducts its expenses in full out of the portion the moviemaker received after the split in profits with the other films. Because they signed a deal that had distribution expenses attached, they most likely will be in the red forever and show that they actually owe the distributor money!

Step Five: The moviemaker won't hear from the distributor for several months and possibly years. Time will go buy, with your reports only barely moving toward paying back your expenses. Plus, by this point the moviemaker's movie is old, and the distributor has many more new, exciting titles to work with. Your reports start to look like duplicates of themselves, because nothing has changed and no money is made.

Step Six: The moviemaker's cast and crew will get excited to see the movie in Walmart, Redbox, and/or Netflix. Meanwhile, the moviemaker is wondering why they still haven't made any money from the distributor. They call the distributor, but no one returns their call.

Step Seven: Five, maybe ten years later, the moviemaker finally gets his or her film back, but it's already super old and nobody cares. Now they can choose to re-sign with the company or do something different. But by this point, they've already given up and moved back home with their parents. Or even worse, taken a day job.

Step Eight: The moviemaker never makes another movie again!

Step Nine: The moviemaker is sad.

Depressing isn't it? And as sarcastic as I make this sound, it's pretty accurate. The good news is that you are reading this book, and you can change this outcome by gaining a little knowledge and confidence.

Never be afraid to walk away from a bad deal. NEVER!

I have a very successful film friend, and his best advice to me was, *"Sometimes the best deals are the ones you walk away from."* Producers get so desperate

215

to sign off their hard work. They lack the self-confidence in knowing how to profit from their dreams and endeavors. It is the reason a corrupt industry has been allowed to flourish and why the problem is systemic. You must train your brain to have faith in the success of your film.

Now, I am not saying you should expect to make a million dollars when you made a movie with your neighborhood friends on a cell phone. I mean, it's possible I suppose, but it's a bit unrealistic. What I'm talking about here is the possibility to get your film on TV, VOD, or shown at a film festival and to make some money while doing it. It's possible, and if you've followed my suggestions in chapter Two regarding budget, then you might even be able to claim a profit from your movie and continue to make more. If a deal does not allow you a mechanism to monetize your valuable content and only offers you a hopeful stab for exposure then it's a bad deal. Walk away!

Finding the right lawyer.

First off, NEVER—and I mean NEVER—sign any deal without consulting a verified and experienced entertainment attorney. Look for a lawyer who has experience in film distribution. Get referrals and do your homework before you retain them. Do not assume that any entertainment lawyer will be useful for your distribution contract.

Some entertainment lawyers specialize in music rights, copyright, or performance rights. The movie business requires a particular set of insights regarding the contract, which a musical-entertainment lawyer may not know about. By default, many legal advisors will look for pitfalls in a distribution contract. Their main objective is to protect the interest of the producer, which is good, but it doesn't help you put provisions in place to keep the distributor honest and fair. This doesn't make them bad lawyers, but it doesn't help you as a producer or filmmaker when it comes to making money.

When you are looking for a movie-entertainment lawyer, especially when it comes to distribution, you need to ask the hard questions:

1. **Have you ever worked on a distribution agreement?**

2. **Do you understand rights management?**

3. **Do you understand how movies are sold in the market?**

4. **Can you help me secure a deal that will maximize my ability to earn money when my movie starts selling?**

By asking these basic questions, it will help you filter out the people who, despite their best intentions, are not suitable for this aspect of your journey.

The contract, good deals vs. bad deals, and what to make sure is in them for yourself.

So here is what a bad deal looks like. I will explain each of these areas subsequently:

BAD DEAL

- Long-term contracts (contracts ranging from four years or more)

- Net deals with expenses

- No definition of gross receipts

- Contracts that take all rights, including ancillary rights, and all territories, and mediums. Also known as *universal-rights grabs.*

- Contracts that allow the distributor to modify your film, title and art

- Contracts that do not allow for auditing the distributor's books

Long-term contracts: Film Distribution companies love having long terms. They will argue that it takes several years to fully exploit an independent movie. This is rubbish. They aim to have long-term contracts, because it allows them to keep large catalogues of titles over longer periods of time. It's a practice that is widely used within the industry and locks creators into ridiculously long-term relationships. The reason they do not need anything longer than three years, is because after your film cycles through two years of markets, the buyers want to see new things. It's more than likely the distributor won't even promote your movie at their booth after the first year, let alone the second year. They keep the film on lockdown, just in case someone comes looking for something particular.

How to negotiate this: As a rule I do not sign any agreement over three years. If a company wants anything longer, I counter it by requesting them to pay a minimum guarantee in advance for every year after the original three-year term. If they say *no way* then you say *Adios*.

Net deals with expenses: Gross deals are the only deal you should sign. Period. Let me say this again. **Gross deals are the only deals you should sign!** Most micro-movie-distribution companies will NOT want to do a gross deal. They enjoy the benefits of adding expenses to the agreement. This is actually how they make their money. These deals are known as expense deals or NET deals. The reason you do not want to sign NET deals is because distributors spend very little money, if any, on the actual marketing of your film. They do not accumulate anymore expenses than they normally do by having your title. In fact, they have office expenses, utilities, staff payroll, and attend film markets regardless if your film is in their catalog or not.

Typically distributors do not pay for advertisements for a particular film title. It's very rare. The cost of advertising a single indie title doesn't make much sense. One advertisement in a trade could cost them anywhere between $5,000-$10,000. If a distribution company does spend money on your film, it's usually in lab fees (to ready your movie for delivery to a buyer) or to create a new poster or trailer. These costs should always be a part of their normal operational expenses and not tied to your movie particularly.

Most NET agreements that I've seen have expenses that range anywhere between $5000 and $30,000 on the average, and in some extreme cases $100,000. With these numbers levied against your film's earnings, it will make it nearly impossible to recoup or earn a dollar on your title. The only way NET deals make money for the moviemaker is if you are super lucky and your little movie goes on to earn hundreds of thousands of dollars. If your film makes a million dollars its first year, then you would see some money back. But you would have a better chance winning the lottery twice.

So how to negotiate this: First and foremost, never be afraid to walk away from a NET deal. They are

222

awful deals, regardless of how much sweet-talk the company dishes at you or how many promises they make. And even if they are a big distribution company, Net Deals are still rubbish.

If you sign this type of a deal, you might as well donate your movie to them for free. When talking with potential distribution partners, I make it very clear from the beginning of the dialogue that my company does not sign NET deals with expenses. Rather, I am always willing to negotiate a smaller percentage of GROSS receipts in exchange for their cooperation. I would suggest doing a 40-60 split or even a 30-70. Either of these will be better than a deal with expenses.

No definition of gross receipts: Getting a distributor to sign up for a Gross deal is just the beginning. Having them define what that means is super important. Without a legal definition of Gross Receipts, the distribution company can exclude and hide various revenue streams from the agreement. Oftentimes, distribution companies work with other distribution companies to release titles. These are known as a *sub-distributors*. Here's an example:

Company B has a deal with Walmart. Company A (your distributor) has a deal with them.

Now it may seem obvious that you should be entitled to earn any money that comes from Company B's profits as a result to selling your movie. That would make sense. Company B also has a separate deal with Company D, in which they split the gross profits with them before sharing anything with Company A, your company. There are certain clauses in distribution agreements where subdistribution monies can be excluded as part of the Gross Receipts. Contracts do this by excluding any language that limits their ability to wheel and deal with potential subdistribution partners. Now that makes sense for the distributor, but the problem you face as the filmmaker is that without any clarity on what is considered "gross revenue," your film's revenue is considered collateral damage for doing business.

An example

When Company A (your distribution company) grants the right for Company B to release your movie, they are also granting them the right to sell your movie in other markets with their own subdistributors. Your movie could end up being three-times removed from your distributor, and neither you nor your own distributor would get any part of those deals. Now you may be asking why Company A would do a deal in which it may exclude them from making any money? Well, the reason is simple: Company A benefits from having close relations with companies like Company B, especially companies that are the gatekeepers to major retail markets like Walmart or Netflix. Although they may not physically profit from allowing their own subdistributors to subdistribute your movie to other parties, they benefit from keeping these companies friendly and allowing them to place their other products in larger markets and major retailers. Think of it as the cost of doing business. So in closing they get the benefit from the relationship at your expense. They are

WHAT FILM SCHOOLS DON'T TELL YOU / SCHWARZE

in fact selling off your movie to a subdistributor to do whatever they want. This is why defining what gross receipts means keeps your hands in every possible transaction and gives you claim to any and all monies a company makes from your film.

Although I am not a lawyer (nor should you copy and paste any of this text into your actual contract), here is what I have defined gross receipts in my past contracts:

Any and all monies derived and generated from the sale, exploitation, transfer, trade, and/or distribution of the motion picture by the distributor and/or by any of the distributor's subdistributors, partners, affiliates, agents and/or representatives and by any other party shall be considered Gross Revenue.

How to negotiate this: Typically this can be an area of conflict in an agreement. Distributors do not like having their hands tied. Some companies will laugh at you and walk away. But do not fear. My experience has told me that if a distributor has agreed to do a gross deal, then they expect there to be a solid definition of gross. It may force them to divulge their operators and strategies more and put limits of the rights they give to their subdistribution partners, but that is okay. If they fuss, then you push back harder than ever. Because without this definition, your hard work fighting for a gross deal is in vain. Add this to your list of non-negotiables.

Contracts that take all rights, including ancillary rights and all territories and mediums. Also known as Universal Rights Grabs.

Never let a distributor take all of your rights. You have to think of every movie as a pizza pie. The pizza can be cut up and served in various shapes to various people. Your movie is no exception. You want to preserve the following rights for yourself or for future distribution potentials.

All Ancillary Rights: These are rights like sequels, books, toys, character-licensing stuff, and merchandise.

Rights to attainable and selfdistributed VOD markets. These are things like Amazon Prime Video or Hulu. You can do these yourself or hire an aggregator.

The right to sell DVDs or digital copies from your website or place of business. Why not? If you have an audience base, why not monetize them directly? No sense in giving up that money.

The expression *Don't put all your eggs in one basket* comes to mind when I think of this point. If you have a bad distribution partner and they own everything during the term of the contract, then you are stuck. You want to give yourself some maneuvering in the event that you need to do something else with your movie. Plus if your movie ends up being a success and your distributor wants the sequel rights, they will have to renegotiate a better deal to get it.

Some distributors love having entire ownership over a property and will refuse to allow you to keep any of it for yourself. They will claim they need all the rights to exploit the picture and do their jobs. But the truth is that they will rarely ever exercise all of these rights and will hold them for no reason.

How to negotiate this: I would start by looking at the rights that you can exercise yourself. These are rights like posting your movie on VOD through Amazon Prime Video, Hulu, iTunes, and/or hiring an aggregator to do it for you. Perhaps you can offer to release some of these rights back to the distributor if they can prove that they do a good job in other areas. Think of it as bargaining chips. Although there are certain buyers that won't take a title if it's been released elsewhere, you can still hold certain rights until success has been proven. You can place a term limit of some of these rights too.

Contracts that allow the distributor to modify your film, title, and art.

You need to make sure that the distributor has to get your approval to re-edit or change your film. Now obviously the distributor may need to edit your film for the sake of commercial breaks or inserting ads or to subtitle or dub your movie in different languages. These are exceptions. But make sure you clarify what they can or cannot do. I suggest asking the agreement to read something like the following:

Distributor and its affiliates shall have the right to edit the motion picture for the sole purpose of inserting commercial breaks, subtitling, and voiceover dubbing, and shall be permitted to create new key-art and promotional videos, including trailers for marketing purposes. No other changes shall be made, including but not limited to changing the title, reediting the movie in part or in whole, changing the names of characters, changing location names, rearranging scenes, color-correcting, changing music, changing graphics, deleting scenes, adding scenes, inserting actors, inserting product placements, and/or any

other alterations to the motion picture without the written approval of the producer.

After all of this is said and done, it would be wise to consult with your distributor to see if changing titles or artwork could benefit the sales of your film. After all, they have a job to do, and you want them to be able to sell your film the best way they know how. I often take the advice of my distribution partners. I want them to have an easier time selling my films, so by allowing them to do certain small changes helps them place the content better.

Contracts that do not allow for auditing the distributor's books:

Most distribution contracts have clauses that allow the filmmaker to audit the books of the distributor, but I felt it was worthy of mention in this chapter. In order to keep your distributor honest, you wish to make sure you have the ability to check the facts. Obviously an audit is something that you should be expected to do yourself, but if the time comes where you feel that you need to exercise this right, you want to make sure you have a good CPA who knows what to look for. I suggest finding a CPA who understands business expenses and has some experience in the entertainment industry. I would suggest making sure the following is included in your agreement.

Producer shall have the right to audit any distributor's financials regarding the motion picture and shall be granted access to any and all invoices, receipts, spreadsheets, copies of deposits from buyers, and any and all transactions made throughout this agreement. Producer will be responsible for paying any audit fees, and all audits must be conducted at the distributor's place of business during normal business hours.

How to negotiate this: If for some crazy reason your agreement doesn't have an audit clause in it, then I would suggest simply adding this to your list of revisions after you counter their initial agreement. If a company is unwilling to allow you to see its financials with regard to your business deal, then they are not trustworthy enough to be entering business with.

How to find a distributor

To most people's surprise, finding a distributor for your film is actually easy; finding a good one is the more challenging process. These companies need you as much as you need them. But you must make sure that the company you are signing with plays fair. You want to find a distribution company that you can be a partner with. A partner that you could possibly grow with.

Partners have equal stake in the outcome of a project's success. If one party has nothing to lose, then it makes for a bad one-sided arrangement, and nothing favorable can be gained by the other party. After all, you made the film. That cost a ton of money, so why should your new partner not have to buy in to win with you? I have spoken with distribution reps who boasted how great they are at selling titles but would never stake their own money on their claims. My thinking is,

233

"If you're that good, then you shouldn't be worried about making your money back."

Some moviemakers that I have stressed this point with have argued, *"But what if it's a big company? If I walk away, then I will not get the exposure."* The flaw with this assumption is that they assume the company will actually do something with their movie. In the old days, producers would get what they called advances or minimum guarantees (MGs), and while some gurus have recently proclaimed that the MGs have returned, most distribution companies want very little risk or skin in the game.

Advances and MGs were payments from the distributor to the producer or producer of a movie, which would later be reimbursed to the distribution company once the movie started making money. However, these days distribution companies have their pick of the litter. They operate in tonnage, meaning they make money by amassing huge volumes of content and placing them in libraries. They may in fact decide to sit on a film title until there is a trend within a particular genre, or if a bigger studio film is released, they may put out films that are similar in scope to ride the popularity of the moment. Either way betting the farm on prestige is an awful gamble that the producer typically loses.

My suggestion would be to look for a distribution company that fits the level and genre of the title you are pushing. If you have a zombie movie, find a company that specializes in horror. If you have a drama, look for companies that fit that demographic. Do not assume that every distributor is the same. They each apply different tactics and strategies to the market.

I typically start my distribution searches via IMDb pro. However, there are tons of tools and lists that you can purchase that give you access to thousands of companies worldwide.

Step One: Make a database using a spreadsheet program so you can keep track of the companies you've contacted. You also want to indicate special notes about each of these companies and whether or not you've spoken with anyone. Also take notice of their response rate. If they are slow getting back to you in the early stages, this problem will only grow as time goes on.

Step Two: Like I mentioned earlier in this chapter, write out an email that you can copy and paste into separate emails. Leave room in these emails to personalize them. Don't send out spam emails to everyone. Perhaps you can reference the person's recent achievements or call out the attention of one of their other titles that you enjoy. Whatever it is you should be engaging and focus the letter more on what they want as a company than what you want as a filmmaker.

Here's an example:

Dear {insert acquisitions person's name here},

First off, thank you for your time. My name is **{insert your name},** and I am with **{insert your**

company name}. I wanted to congratulate you on all the success you are having with **{insert their company name}** and in particular the recent release of **{insert their movie title here}**, which I just saw on **{insert where you saw their movie}**. The film was really enjoyable, and the production value was fantastic. This was one of my main inspirations for reaching out to you.

My company is currently looking for distribution partners for our recent film **{insert your movie title here}** and wanted to see if it was a good fit for your company's portfolio. **{Insert your title here}** is a **{insert a two sentence description of your movie}**. It was filmed primarily in **{insert some production info here, such as location and anything notable that could be of value to the overall production}**. If this is something you would be interested in looking at, you can see the film's trailer at **{insert a link to your film's trailer}**. From there, I can send you a password-protected link to view the entire film.

Thank you in advance for your time and consideration. I look forward to hearing from you.

{insert your name and contact info here}

If you notice, I didn't even mention the title of the movie I was pitching until the second paragraph. Pointing out the positive things the recipient is interested in is the most important thing. This is Sales 101 stuff here. Moreover, you will notice my letter was very brief, less than three paragraphs. Plus, my tone was empathetic to their time. This is another area that you must be conscious of. Most acquisitions people are inundated with emails and letters. Some filmmakers even have the gal to send screeners without getting their recipient's permission. The goal of this first query is to open a chain of dialogue and hopefully get the prospective company interested in your title.

And so they respond:

Hey filmmaker,

Thanks for the kind words. Yes. Please send us a link to see the movie. :-)

Acquisitions person

After you have received a reply back requesting the full-movie screener, then you should send them the finished version. Let me stress if your movie is not 100 percent completed, do NOT send them a copy or link. Some companies will say, *"We understand if it's not complete. We look at these kinda things all the time. We get it."* Don't be so eager. Wait until you get the film done 100 percent. Bad sound or color correction will not help your case, regardless of how astute the acquisition person may claim to be. If the sound is bad, then that's what they will remember. Send them your very best.

Step Three: Send a secure screener link or DVD to the company right away. If they like the movie, then they will reply back.

Hey filmmaker,

Really enjoyed your movie. Good sound and the production was spot on. We would like to offer you distribution through our company.

Please see the attached distribution agreement. Please let me know if you have any questions. Thanks again.

Acquisitions person

Step Four: Start the negotiating process. They said they like your title. Now it's about trying to figure out how much they like your title, or if they are simply trying to take advantage of the situation. If they've rushed to send over their boilerplate agreement, then I would follow up with this response:

240

Hello Acquisitions person,

Thank you so much for the quick reply and the consideration for distributing our movie. We are humbled that you enjoyed the movie. It really means a lot. I looked through the agreement and saw a few areas that I would like to address. Would you have any time this week to discuss?

Thank you again.

Acquisitions person

Step Five: You wait for their response. Meanwhile, you should be performing steps one through three with a dozen other companies.

Step Six: You receive a response. More than likely there are some litigious points they are countering. Nonetheless, this is where you inject the consul of an experienced movie-distribution entertainment lawyer. You give them your following

241

points, which we described above, and ask them to go over these items in detail. From this point forward, you should have your lawyer involved with all of the communication.

Hopefully after a few tweaks, you will secure a deal that makes sense for you and for the distributor. If you can negotiate all of these points, then you are well within reach of setting the course for financial reward. This is of course is if your distribution partner does their job. Hopefully you have a short term deal, so if it's a stinker, you can get out of it faster.

Deliverables:

Once you have signed off your film to a distributor, you will be asked to deliver the following items. There might be more, but for the sake of this exercise, I would like the point out the most common and important

M&E tracks: These are music and effects-tracks that exclude any dialogue. This allows the distributor to dub the picture in other languages without losing the music or effects layers. If you do not have these, then you need to get with your editor immediately to arrange these items. It's best to think of keeping your editing timeline clean and organized through the postproduction process, so you can easily bounce out these various tracks after your movie is completed.

Music Cue Sheet: Music cue sheets are time code-based documents that help the distributor make sure the music timing stays on point. Sometimes when a movie is being edited for commercial breaks or dubbing voiceovers in different languages, the music tracks can be knocked out of sync. The music cue sheet can be referenced in order to make sure nothing gets messed up.

Copyright from Library of Congress: Having a copyright of your script or completed film is very important. You should do both actually. Sometimes authors will register their scripts with the Writers Guild of America (WGA), which is cool too, but the official copyright is needed in order for a company to solicit your intellectual property. Think of it more as proof that you are the owner of the material.

Dialogue Sheet: Much like the music cue sheet, a dialogue sheet is used not only for timing but subtitling and dubbing. These documents should give the time code and dialogue for every single word and should also give the character's name. I typically have my team modify the screenplay with only the dialogue and have them associate the time code for each line.

Key Art: Key art, movie posters, one sheets—it's all the same these days. However, you should provide your distributor a large and layered Photoshop file of your poster art. Typically one sheets are 27" x 41" and at least 200 DPI resolution. Most VOD platforms have their own size requirements, so the distributor needs to have the ability to change and rearrange your key art to fit these other sizes. You can also request that you do these requirements yourself.

244

Movie Trailer: It goes without saying, you need a movie trailer. Now, I'm not talking about a trailer you tow behind a truck. I'm talking about a preview, commercial, advertisement of your movie. Making a movie trailer is very difficult and can be a daunting task for most moviemakers. At the end of your movie project you are exhausted, and the last thing you want to do is cut the thing down to a two-minute preview. My suggestion is find a big-budget movie trailer that you like and one that fits the genre of film you are making. From there, dissect it and make detailed notes of when the cuts happen and the types of shots and dialogue they use. Then basically emulate the trailer beat for beat, and you will discover that even your little micro-budget movie can look like a million bucks.

W-9: Anytime someone is going to give you money in the United States, you need to submit a W-9 form to that payee. This allows them to issue your tax information at the end of the year. If you are a limited liability company (LLC) or corporation, then you would use your employer identification number (EIN). Otherwise you will need to submit your Social Security number on this form. Always check with a certified accountant if you are unclear about tax information.

Digital masters of the film: The final deliverable is obviously the most important. You must deliver your new distribution partner the highest quality version of your film. If you shoot in 4K or 6K, you need to make sure they have that version as well. I always send 4K masters as well as 1080 (high definition) versions of my movie. Most of the time, they only use the 1080 version, but some buyers are now requesting media to be delivered in at least 4K resolution. Be sure to get a list of deliverable requirements and specs from your distributor.

Film Premiere and Public Screenings

The term *theatrical release* sounds so sexy to indie moviemakers. Let's be real, there is nothing cooler than watching your movie on the silver screen. There is something magical about it. Some distributors will utilize a four-wall strategy (meaning they rent the four walls of a theater to show a movie) in efforts to add value to a film's release potential.

For example, some prestigious VOD outlets will not acquire original content unless it's had a *theatrical run*. In order to get around this hurdle, some distributors will purchase screens in selected cities to qualify it as a national theatrical run. In any event there may be additional deliverables that are required for screening in a theatrical environment. You may need to provide your distributor a Digital Cinema Package (DCP) in order for them to show your movie at these theaters.

Old Models Versus New

It's safe to say that by the time you read this book, there will already be a dozen or more new alternatives for the indie film-distribution space. It changes nearly each quarter. Some new platform opens and filmmakers rush in to capitalize on the market share. That said, the objective of the

247

subsequent text is to offer you a little brain fodder for the alternatives for distribution. That said, there are benefits to both traditional and DIY indie film distribution. Let's explore:

Traditional Distribution Company

There are advantages and disadvantage to traditional distribution. One of the biggest advantages is that you can reach a wider release potential with your film. The reason for this is that many sales companies and distribution firms have established relationships with buyers worldwide. It makes it easier for them to get movies into the international marketplace. Moreover, the foreign-film market by large is based on relationships. When you partner with a distribution company, that is what you are essentially paying for.

A traditional distributor can also find creative money-making opportunities where there might be little to no competition. For example, the Turks and Caicos Islands have a big demand for action movies since launching a new TV network. Most likely only a

248

distribution company would have access to that early information and would be the best tool in brokering a conversation with the stakeholders of the network. Moreover, in some cases having an established distributor can also help your funding opportunities with private investors. Some investors want to know distribution is in place before they put money in. Plus, having a distributor can add legitimacy to your production.

Some of the disadvantages of going the traditional-distribution route has been pointed out earlier in this chapter. However, the biggest pitfall I have seen with handing over all of your film's rights to a company is that you as the filmmaker do not learn anything about the market. It's easy to place yourself into the mind-set that it's someone else's job to sell, but by holding on to and exercising your territorial rights, it forces you to have a better understanding of what is needed to make a film project a success. Knowing the market helps you become a better producer and commercial filmmaker.

DIY Distribution

The advantages of DIY indie distribution may seem obvious: You get to keep your rights. You don't have to sign nasty contracts with sales companies. You get to make 100 percent profit off your film when it starts to earn money. But the biggest advantage in DIY distribution is that you can learn to start positioning yourself as a brand. You also learn a great deal from your audience.

However, DIY distribution should not be attempted by the those who are lazy. Doing it yourself requires a lot of work. There are a few disadvantages to this model. The biggest one is that you will need to make sure you can place your content on Video-on-demand (VOD) platforms without the aid of a distribution company. Some platforms require you to work through an aggregator.

An aggregator is a preferred quality-control company that specializes in brokering content and managing quality control for the platforms. They usually charge a flat up-front fee and allow you to keep all of your earnings once you get onto the platform and start earning money. Over the last few years, aggregators have become increasingly popular and have given rise to an influx of independent producers and filmmakers creating their own distribution companies. In my opinion, hiring an aggregator is a great tool but should only be a portion of your overall strategy.

Another item of caution when doing your own distribution is marketing. When you work with a distributor, they don't necessarily market your movie. They use what the industry calls *positioning*. This means they position your movie for success on shelves and on VOD by making the artwork look good, and in some cases changing the title and brokering better placement. Aggregators typically do not do this for you. It will be up to you to use clever marketing strategies in order for people to find your content. In short, you may be able to get your film onto a platform like Amazon, but how is anyone going to know it's there?

251

In the next chapter, I will outline a few various marketing strategies for you. But before we move on, here is a quick list of pros and cons for both traditional and DIY distribution:

PROS FOR TRADITIONAL DISTRIBUTION:

- *Better product placement in stores*

- *Access to brick and mortar stores and retail outlets*

- *Legitimacy with investors*

- *Less concern over marketing and sales*

CONS OF TRADITIONAL DISTRIBUTION:

- *Bad deals (net deals with expenses)*

- *Long-terms contracts*

- *Having to trust the company to do their jobs*

- *No guarantee on anything*

- *Having to share profits (if any) with the sales company indefinitely*

- *Not making some money from subdistributors*

- *Have to give up your rights*

- *You have little control over the branding of your film*

PROS FOR DIY DISTRIBUTION:

- You keep your rights.

- You keep 100 percent of your profits.

- You have control over your product's branding and presentation.

- You can learn about the marketplace.

CONS OF DIY DISTRIBUTION:

- You have more work.

- You have to market your own film.

- Sometimes you have to pay upfront fees to aggregators.

- You can't reach some markets that a traditional distributor can sell to.

- It may be seen as a higher risk for investment.

Now after reading this, you may still be puzzled as to which direction is best for your film's future. Of course your options may vary based on the situation and terms you can establish with your traditional distributor, but allow me to offer you the best possible model for your micro movie.

Kelly's best model for indie film distribution

Traditional Distribution Portion

1. *Sign a "gross deal" with a traditional-distribution company. This means, NO expenses with a definition of gross receipts.*

2. *Short term deal, three years.*

3. *You keep your AVOD, SVOD, and TVOD rights for at least iTunes, Amazon, Hulu, Google Play, or any other platform you can reach via an aggregator.*

4. *Keep your rights to sell DVDs or digital downloads from your own storefront.*

5. *You control all branding and films' presentation.*

DIY Distribution Portion

1. *Hire an aggregator to place you on the VOD platforms that make the most sense for your film.*

2. *Create a storefront for your film and sell directly to your fan base and supporters through that platform.*

3. *Build an email list that you can market to.*

In closing this chapter, I would suggest that you start having conversations early with distributors. Try to form relationships. In the end your success will depend on a multi-prong approach. You must learn to master all of the relationship hurdles of business. Do not turn your back on one option. Always look to evolve your strategy and be open minded. In the end, if you adhere to all of the basic precautions I have listed in this chapter, you will most likely discover success with indie-film distribution.

Marketing against the noise

Let me be clear. I am not a marketing genius, nor do I profess to be a master on the subject. But what I can speak to is the fact that over the last ten years, movie marketing has changed. The ability to reach audiences has changed. In yesteryears, most moviegoers couldn't be reached without the aid of television, radio, or newspapers. Hollywood monopolized the industry because it could buy out radio and newspaper ad buys.

Today, filmmaking at any level can attract, cultivate, and mobilize customers via the internet as long as it has the right message and strategy. Despite all the wiz-bang and trendy tools of marketing these days, many moviemakers are still falling short on maximizing their market potential. Moreover, most advertising efforts fall to a blind eye as many are tuning out the clutter they see. In my business I employ old and new techniques in order to rise above the noise. My strategy has seemed to work over the last few years both on the filmmaking and services' side of my business. It has helped my wife and me launch a successful indie-film studio and has placed me at the top of my local filmmaking community.

The little studio in the desert

Content creators like myself are now realizing that it's not just about racking up Likes, followers, or subscribers; it's about building a slow and steady consciousness of our entire body of work. Sometimes this body of work transcends filmmaking and bridges other areas of our business. Take for example, the Indie Film Factory. The studio was founded by Charisma Manulat, my wife and business partner. At the time we started the company, I was already partners in a small video-production firm. I remember coming home one day and Charisma telling me that she wanted to open a studio for indie filmmakers. Now I have to be honest, I thought the idea was horrible when I first heard it.

"Why would you do that?" I thought. *"Filmmakers are always broke!"*

But what Charisma knew—and I was ignorant of—was the importance of community. She wasn't looking at the studio as a business model. She saw it as a place, a clubhouse to cultivate creative talent. She came up with a mission statement that read:

Indie Film Factory is an affordable studio created specifically for indie filmmakers. Our mission is to encourage our filmmaking community

to create quality films and to build a positive culture of teaching, learning, and growth. Make your movie!

I immediately started to wonder how this new business would tie into our other projects, particularly our movies. For years I had approached each movie project separately as a stand-alone marketing campaign, not fully realizing the power of brand and audience building.

Charisma founded the Indie Film Factory in December 2011, and much to our surprise, the local film community was very supportive. We launched with a huge party, and overnight we became the new, cool place for local producers. And within a few months, we not only were attracting local moviemakers, but even major TV shows, film producers, and some of the biggest entertainment companies in the world.

As time progressed, while we continued to produce new movies, we started to notice a trend. People who were clients of our studio also become devoted fans of our film projects. Moreover, clients who were looking to rent a studio when they came into town trusted us more because we actually made movies. The studio side and movie company both benefited from this relationship. A brand was slowly forming, and we dedicated ourselves to be a community.

At the time we didn't realize it, but we had built a brand around ourselves as moviemakers with the spirit in which we did things. People weren't coming to see our movies because they were motivated by slick trailers or our social-media marketing skills. They were coming to support us because of our mission statement. At the core of our mission, is independence. It's freedom from Hollywood, freedom from financial constraint, independence from anyone telling us what we can do, and the enlightenment that people can do anything. This message is not particular to our trade. It can be meaningful and inspiring to any industry. It calls for people to take action and believe in themselves.

Today when we release movies, I think of them more as extensions of that core mission statement. It's evidence of that belief. Despite being outside of Hollywood or having illustrious budgets to burn through, we create regardless, sometimes with great results and other times not so much. But it doesn't matter. People like that about us, and it doesn't matter if we fall short or not. We are doers. Period. Nothing will stop us from *doing*, and people within our community know that and rally behind us.

I draw your attention to this example not to say that you need another business in order to build a brand. The business is inconsequential. It's the message and charter you set up for yourself that's most important. Your mission could be anything from the following list:

1. *To make movies free from the chains of Hollywood*

2. *To take audiences to other worlds, times, and adventures*

3. *To be the cinematic voice for social awareness and change*

WHAT FILM SCHOOLS DON'T TELL YOU / SCHWARZE

4. To make movies that scare the pants off people

5. Activism through the lens

6. To inspire female empowerment

7. To create the best entertainment for children

Sound too lofty? Think about this for a second. The most famous filmmakers in history created their brands from this list whether they deliberately did so or not.

1. Francis Ford Coppola: Founder of American Zoetrope

2. George Lucas: Star Wars, Indiana Jones

3. Ava DuVernay: Salem, A Wrinkle In Time, 13th

4. Alfred Joseph Hitchcock: Strangers on a Train, The Birds, Rear Window, Psycho

5. Michael Francis Moore: Bowling for Columbine, Where to Invade Next

6. Patty Jenkins: Wonder Woman, Monster

7. Walter Elias Disney, Founder of Walt Disney Studios

Each of these mavericks are examples of a defined action plan. They had a major purpose and a vision of their brand long-term. Now some of these may seem obvious to you, ***just make the kind of films you want to make.*** But until you fully understand the value of creating a core message, a mission statement, and purpose for yourself as content creators, you cannot build a community or inspire a conversation with your content.

How to start building an audience starts with finding your core message. It's often advised that young novelists stay within genres. The reason for this advice is that each work you create plays into the values of your audience. You start to build followers and support by building consistency. I can speak to this first hand. When I started my career, I was all over the map. I

263

made a comedy, a drama, then back to comedy, then thriller, then science fiction. But my last two movies stayed close to the same theme and genre. Although, one was a science-fiction film with a monster and the other was a movie about a nasty chemical weapon, both played into the interests of those who are curious about the *military-industrial complex*. Both of these movies were designed to ask the question, "How much does our government keep from its people?" That said, we quickly garnered support from one film to the next, and it has offered an interesting spillover from one movie to the next.

Here are some basic things you could do to get the ball rolling with your branding and audience building.

Establish a mission statement for yourself as a filmmaker.

Start to map out the types of stories you want to tell.

Start a website, social-media presence, and way to blog about your journey as a content creator. This includes showing behind the scenes and other video and image content that allows your audience to form a relationship with you as a creative.

Once the movie is complete, host local trailer-release parties and press events. These can be very simple and should reflect the type of character you are. If you are a self-funded moviemaker, then you can do these events as humble as money will allow.

Map out your release schedule with your distributor. Plan to release your movie in each territory or platform in conjunction with their plans. Keep in mind that some buyers will want exclusivity on releases, and you must work with your sales company to plan these things out.

By taking these few baby steps with your plan, you can garner a great deal of awareness and support by the time your movie comes out.

CHAPTER 10
Are film festivals really worth it?

A few years ago I attended a film festival in Temecula, California, where I had a movie premiering. A week prior to the event, the festival organized a filmmaker mixer at a local winery. Three of the cast members and I jumped in a car and drove up from Las Vegas for the occasion. When we arrived we noticed that despite being a networking event, NO ONE WAS NETWORKING. Moviemakers were huddled into little groups and seemed nervous to engage with each other. Right away my star and I hit the bar, and after a few glasses of the good stuff, we went to work. The actor and I split the room. I took one side while he took the other. We engaged creators directly, not by telling them about our film, but asking them to talk about theirs. The results were astonishing. By the end of the night, we had managed to create a huge chatterbox of conversations, not one of them regarding our movie.

266

We ended up taking flyers and contact information on everyone we had met.

A week later, we arrived back in Temecula for the actual festival. Our film was scheduled for two screenings later in the week. Although we had at least a few days to settle in and check out other creatives' work, we went to the festival's filmmaker lounge and asked people if they needed help promoting their screenings while we were there. To their surprise, we offered to pass out handbills and engage people outside the theaters where the movies were playing. Keep in mind that most of these filmmakers were by themselves, so by offering to be an extension of their support staff, it was unprecedented.

As promised, my team, which included my wife, three of the actors, and our executive producer, took the task of helping our fellow filmmakers promote their screenings. We handed out flyers and spoke with people about the other films that were screening that week. The response was magnificent. We managed to help a handful of films reach full capacity for their screenings. After a few days of festivities, we had also met some really great and talented artists, most of whom I still remain friends with to this day.

It finally came time to showcase our world premiere. I was nervous, and the cast and crew were a little nervous too. We had spent a great deal of time helping others promote their work and very little time helping get the word out about our own movie. We took advantage of a festival party, and we did our best to promote our upcoming screening. I would be lying if I told you I wasn't nervous about filling the seats. However, despite all of our concerns, something magical happened. The filmmakers whom we had helped promote the days leading up to our screenings, tossed their marketing materials aside and pounded the streets for our little movie. We had close to eight different film groups working the theater lobby and filmmaker lounge on our behalf. Fifteen minutes after the doors opened to our world premiere, there wasn't a seat left. We sold out the house. We had people from every section of society. There were moviemakers, Temecula locals, and even some folks who had decided to watch our movie rather than seeing the Hollywood movie they went there to see initially. The screening went off without a hitch. Total success, and the crowd loved it. The Q&A went on for nearly thirty minutes after the movie ended, and the questions followed all the way to the front entrance of the theater. We had managed to create an amazing turnout simply by helping other creators achieve their goals. And what was even more incredible, the second screening later that weekend was nearly at full capacity too.

After the festival ended, we went back to Las Vegas feeling that we had conquered the very essence of the festival experience. We returned home with no distribution contract or any fancy awards to show, but we racked up a wide list of friends and colleagues who went on to help us champion the film afterward.

The moral of this tale is to point out that film festivals—despite being misinterpreted by many moviemakers—are great ways to network and market yourself. Use them for that! Period.

After the Temecula Festival experience we went on to self-distribution for our movie. We did various online campaigns and local DVD parties and made our money back within a summer. Most of the buzz surrounding our film was due in part to the actions we had taken at the festival. We had established a conversation around our film and had direct access to a base of people.

To use a film festival correctly, one must approach it with a desire to learn, share, and support. It is so tragic when I attend festivals and see directors who will sit through their own screenings but who will leave the second it finishes. I have seen filmmakers leave the theater after their film's credits start to roll, never taking time to support their fellow filmmaker who has a screening up next. It's a sad and selfish tragedy that I feel really stifles our creative community and hurts us all as indie filmmakers.

Film festivals at their core are networking and marketing events. They are also designed to expose moviemakers to each other's ideas and works. If you are lucky enough to get your movie into a film festival, regardless of how big or small it is, use the opportunity to support others, network, and build long-term relationships with others. Go in selflessly and you will discover that a world of success awaits you.

I do want to point out, however, the misconceptions many filmmakers have about film festivals. Let's look at some of these:

- Getting into a film festival (even the big ones) will guarantee me distribution. WRONG

- The more laurel leaves I have on the cover of my poster, the more impressive it will look to a distributor. THEY TYPICALLY COULDN'T CARE LESS

- I need to get into Sundance, SXSW, Toronto, or Cannes in order to be successful. YOU DO NOT

- I should submit to as many festivals as I can and see what happens. TOO EXPENSIVE

Many producers are still thinking in the past when it comes to film festivals. I find it hilarious when a filmmaker's business plan consists of *making a movie and getting it into that Goliath festival.* They would have better luck winning the lottery or becoming a US president. It is so hard to get into Goliath festivals, and many of the micro movies that do manage to sneak in still have a long road ahead of them in finding the right distribution and market success.

The myth associated with film festivals is *you need them to find a distributor and to gain exposure.* This myth has been endorsed, cultivated, and promoted by the film-festival industry. Keep in mind the film-festival industry is a multi-billion-dollar business that profits on the hundreds and sometimes thousands of nonrefundable submissions it takes in every year. Moreover, the festival industry also thrives on sponsorship money and advertisement revenue. Not to say that all festivals are money-making machines, but understand that the culture of film festivals is a business.

Most film festivals, which seem to pop up more and more each week, are not going to impact your film's commercial bottom line. You will not receive any more distribution opportunities than you would working your IMDb distributor's list. In fact, trying to grind out a festival run with your film with the aim to find distribution is craziness: It is expensive and will not benefit your efforts.

So why even submit to a film festival? Well the answer lies in my story above. When we submitted to the Temecula Valley International Film Festival, we knew that it would be easy for us to get to. Plus, it would offer us a backyard advantage to selling ourselves and making new friends nearby. Although the film festival wasn't at the same cache as Sundance or SXSW, this little festival gave us such an incredible experience and helped us launch our movie into the self-distribution marketplace. Had we aimed to get into an East Coast festival, we would not have been able to mobilize the team we needed to make the experience a success.

Case in point. About six years prior to the Temecula experience, we had a movie premiere at a festival in West Palm Beach, Florida. Five of our crew, including myself, attended the festival. Because of the travel expense, we were only able to fly in a day before our movie screened and were not able to stay through the entire festival. Despite our best marketing efforts, we fell short. In the end, my crew and I flew nearly three thousand miles to watch a private screening of our own film. No one showed up! The experience was not only a huge waste of money (nearly $3000 for flight, hotel, and food for the team), but we benefited absolutely nothing from it. No one cared that the movie showed at that festival. There was no gain whatsoever, other than the bonding time I had with my team.

To create a proper film-festival strategy, the best thing to do is look for festivals that are regional to you. Find venues and festivals that you can get to easily, and perhaps be able to bring crew and support with you. Moreover, having the ability to be on the ground a few days before your movie shows is huge. Engage other filmmakers and try to lend support. You have to remember, these people are just like you. In fact, some of them might be from different countries and have no support on the ground. By extending support to others, you will surely find mutual cooperation and start to build a community around yourself as a moviemaker. It's never about the movie itself. It's about the people and ideas behind the movie; keep that in mind.

Do not waste money on top-tier festivals unless your film has the quality and narrative to do so. I am not saying to skip submission to any particular festival, but you must be realistic. I would suggest that many micro-budget movies (movies made for $50,000 or less) will waste money on their submission fees because they are unrealistic with the level of quality and content of their film. My suggestion is to be specific to the type of movie you are making. Find festivals that align their values, themes, scope, and production quality with your movie. If you have a documentary on dogs, perhaps look for festivals that are documentary based or animal themed. I am sure there are some.

If you have a genre movie (horror, action, comedy, thriller, and/or sci-fi), find festivals that specialize in those genres. If you shot your movie on your mobile phone and you made it with some friends from school, don't be heartbroken when it fails to be selected to screen in Park City. Pick yourself up and find a film festival that specializes in movies filmed on cell phones on micro budgets. I know they exist.

In order to maximize success with your festival experience, you need a strategy. Sit down and write out your goals, then see which festival path you want to take. You may also discover that there is a gem of a festival right under your nose and even in your own city.

276

Use your festival money wisely. Sometimes the smaller niche festival is your best bet. Don't throw money away!

Epilogue

I often advise my students to think of their filmmaking careers as lifestyles. Filmmaking is a lifestyle more than anything. It's a way of being, a way of communicating. Without it you feel lost and unheard. My main goal in life is to bring the struggles of the industry down to a level where moviemakers can thrive at any level. If you desire to make a movie, then you should have the right and the ability to do so.

As content creators, the first question that crosses our minds when we consider a project is this: "How are we going to pay for it?" It's a realistic question and one that needs to be addressed before you can really move forward with a project. Most times, producers fall into despair. I mean let's face it, if finances were easy to come by with filmmaking, everyone would be doing movies. The movie industry is designed to be difficult. It's not for the faint of heart. It's

278

designed for those who like the challenge of art and commerce. It's designed for warriors of perseverance and faith. You must have faith in yourself to succeed at this career. You have to believe in yourself even when the world around you doesn't. Rejection, praise, humiliation, and honor all go together in this crazy circus called the movie business. One cannot exist without the others, and sometimes your biggest accomplishments can be counted on one set of fingers.

But regardless of anything, never lose sight of yourself. Find a way to create. Never let budget, politics, people, war, tragedy, poverty, ill health, or any other undesirable circumstance stop you from communicating from the lens. What you have to offer may be a gift. You may reach someone today or someone who is yet to be born. But always remember that your voice needs to be heard.

With that, I leave you. I hope this text will serve as a guide and a textbook to the faithful that you really can have success with your movie career, and it won't require millions of dollars or the fuss of Hollywood.

Be great. Just make movies!

Kelly's Basic Glossary Terms

AC - Assistant Camera (Operator)

AD - Assistant Director

AVOD - Ad-based Video on Demand. The streaming service places advertisements into the film or TV show. This typically allows the viewer to watch content for free. Examples of this are services such as YouTube.

B ROLL - Referring to video coverage filmed to cover up interviews, or primary footage (A Roll).

DP - Director of Photography

SVOD - Subscription Video on Demand. This is where a person pays a subscription to watch movies.

TVOD - Transactional Video on Demand. This is when a person pays a fee to rent or watch a movie on a streaming service.

UPM - Unit Production Manager

VOD - General term referring to Video on Demand, this includes streaming services such as Netflix and Amazon.

JOIN OUR FILMMAKING COMMUNITY

www.indiefilmfactory.com

@iffactory

facebook.com/indiefilmfactory.com

www.ingramcontent.com/pod-product-compliance
Lightning Source LLC
Chambersburg PA
CBHW022003090426
42741CB00007B/870